CW00730783

A HISTORY OF THE
SOVEREIGN

A HISTORY OF THE SOVEREIGN

CHIEF COIN OF THE WORLD

Kevin Clancy

A Royal Mint Museum publication

First published in Great Britain in 2015
Published by the Royal Mint Museum
Llantrisant, Pontyclun CF72 8YT
United Kingdom

www.royalmintmuseum.org.uk

Images copyright as attributed

ISBN 978-1-869917-00-5

A CIP catalogue record for this book is available from the British Library

Designed by Tuch, London

Printed in the United Kingdom by Gavin Martin Colournet Ltd, London

Images of coins are reproduced at actual size unless otherwise stated

Front Cover. Obverse of Henry VII sovereign, 1489; reverse of George III sovereign, 1817
and obverse of Elizabeth II sovereign, 2015 (enlarged)

Frontispiece. Obverse of Henry VII sovereign of 1489 (enlarged)

The
Royal
Mint
MUSEUM

Foreword

Professor Sir David Cannadine

On the sixth of January each year a service is held at the Chapel Royal in London to mark the Feast of the Epiphany, and on behalf of the Queen the traditional gifts of gold, frankincense and myrrh, originally presented by the three kings to the infant Christ in the stable at Bethlehem, are offered up on the altar. For as long as anyone can remember, the golden treasure in question has invariably been presented in the doubly appropriate form of sovereign coins. Here is a vividly telling illustration of how money that was first minted more than five hundred years ago in the reign of Henry VII, and was closely associated with the monarch and the royal court, remains firmly embedded in what remains today of that earlier world.

But the story of sovereign specie has always involved more than the hallowed giving of royal benefactions, for as Sir John Clapham pointed out, writing in 1932, just after Britain had left the Gold Standard, during the nineteenth-century era of Britain's world dominance, the gold sovereign was 'the chief coin of the world'. Across the centuries and around the globe, many monarchies and states, nations and empires, have issued gold coins; but in Britain, as Clapham rightly noted, the high point of the gold sovereign's importance as both a national and international currency was during the sixty years following the Great Exhibition of 1851. It was by no means the only or necessarily the most important form of payment but, as the seemingly dependable embodiment of the Gold Standard and of Britain's global pre-eminence, it underpinned the international financial system until 1914, and again briefly from 1925 to 1931.

A century after the First World War began, and more than eighty years since Britain left the Gold Standard, there is no member of the adult population of the United Kingdom, myself included, who has any personal experience of having carried round in their purse or in their pocket, as our forebears did, a handful of gold sovereigns which were the nation's currency and legal tender – although the single band of my mother's wedding ring (she married like so many wartime brides just after hostilities ceased in 1945) was made from gold sovereigns that her parents had kept since their own marriage for that very purpose. So while sovereigns are still being produced for collectors and for the bullion market, they are no longer common currency that we might receive as change in a supermarket or post office.

But in seeking to understand that once living but now vanished history, we might wonder how wealthy a country would have needed to have been to invest in issuing a coinage of gold; or what technology would have been required to strike it, to mint it and to make it; or who were the artists who designed and fashioned such objects according to (or in defiance of?) the tastes of the time. And we might be concerned, more broadly, to ask how monarchs and politicians sought to have sovereigns made to their own designs; how such coins became essential definers of national culture and signifiers of national identity, and how wars and economic crises have overwhelmed what seemed to have been the most impregnable of fiduciary systems, scattering precious metal coinages like dried leaves or confetti.

It is from such many, varied, stimulating and appropriate perspectives that Dr Kevin Clancy has approached the subject of the five-hundred-year history of the English (then British) gold sovereign. Through a multi-layered narrative he explores the complex and changing relationship between wages, prices and money, he reflects on who the people were in society who might have had access to gold coins, and he wonders what purposes, beyond the purely monetary, were served by such coveted items of high value. From one perspective, sovereigns were an integral part of domestic transactions and international trade; but they were also used by diplomats and courtiers as well as by bankers and merchants, and for rather different purposes; and when not being buried in the ground or hypnotically admired, sovereigns have also been used to seal deals and save British spies. Here, then, is a compelling story, about the (literally) golden age of English and British currency, but also of much more besides.

Below. A stack of gold nobles of Edward III from the mid-fourteenth century (enlarged).

Top. The unsuccessful but attractively designed gold penny of Henry III first struck in 1257.

Above. Florins produced in the northern Italian city state of Florence were amongst the most popular gold coins during the second half of the thirteenth century.

Below. Double-leopards of Edward III, 1344, were struck for only a few months partly because their value had been set too high in relation to the amount of gold the coins contained.

Introduction

Gold as coinage

From the very origins of coinage gold has been part of the story. It provided a portable means through which value could be expressed and by which exchanges could be made. But while the monetary use of this most precious of metals can be understood, and came to be accepted by many civilisations across time and distance, the sacred and venerated qualities of gold have often added another dimension to its role as currency.

The first gold coins to be made in Britain date from more than 2000 years ago. Produced in southern England, their use was probably intermittent and their circulation patchy but they nevertheless formed part of a recognised monetary system. Gold was an element of the circulation of coins in Roman Britain and for several decades in seventh-century Anglo-Saxon England there was an exclusively gold coinage of thrymsas. Silver more often than not, however, predominated in the centuries that followed and the few gold coins to have come to light, such as the discovery in 2001 of a gold mancus of Coenwulf (796-821), have consequently caused quite a stir. Access to regular supplies of gold defined its status in any one territory and in Britain, without meaningful repositories, availability almost always relied on trade, gifts or piracy, or a combination of all three. An economy finding itself with a larger amount of precious metal soon discovered ways in which it could be employed and once the flow became reliable gold often played a role as currency.

Attempts by Henry III (1216-72) to introduce a gold penny were to be undone by lack of demand, and probably by over-valuing the coin in relation to silver, but elsewhere in Europe coinages of gold had started to find their feet, most notably with the florin of Florence and, slightly later in the thirteenth century, the Venetian ducat. The gold in question was coming from west Africa and its passage through commercially powerful Italian city states in sufficient quantities made its transformation into coinage a logical step. In the coming decades similar initiatives were taken by a number of western European countries, such that by the mid-fourteenth century there was a pool of gold coins circulating across the Continent. Familiarity with designs fostered acceptance beyond a specific jurisdiction and a broadly shared commonality of size, weight and value meant that over the course of half a century gold successfully made the transition from altar to purse.

As far as England was concerned, merchants had come to rely on the gold issued by other states for securing larger transactions and it was not until 1344, during the reign of Edward III (1327-1377), that a regular coinage of gold became established and the balance between weight and value was more correctly fixed. The initial series, known as leopards, contrasted markedly with the simple design of the silver coinage. On the double-leopard the king, enthroned, is delicately drawn and on the leopard the Royal Arms of England billow from the collar of a crowned lion, representing the first appearance of heraldry on English coins. Despite their beauty, however, the high value assigned to them meant they were not successful and within a few months they were replaced by the noble which, after a false start, found stability at 6s 8d. As a denomination it worked out at the sensible amount of a third of a pound or half a mark, a mark being 13s 4d or 160d, and was issued alongside its half at 3s 4d and its quarter at 1s 8d. While its value had been pitched at the right level in relation to its gold content, looked at another way it was a profoundly impractical item to employ in the buying and selling of goods: being extremely thin it could easily be bent and being made to a standard of 23 carats 3.5 grains, or 994.8

fine, it would have worn quickly. Its circulation, though, was likely to have been specific rather than general. From the 1350s the highest value silver coin was the groat at fourpence and for most people a noble must have had the air of an exotic creature.

A possible context of usage is provided by rates of pay at the time. In the mid-fourteenth century a building craftsman, such as a carpenter, was paid about fivepence a day which could have equated to an annual salary of about £4. Farming labourers would have regarded in the region of threepence a day as acceptable and could have expected annually to earn somewhat over £2. At a time when food, lodgings, clothes and gratuities of various kinds could well form part of how remuneration was made up, and when the number of days worked during the course of a year could vary significantly, it is by no means easy to arrive at overall levels of income. Master builders, for example, were given fur robes and their subordinates received skins, gloves, aprons, boots and hoods, articles of clothing that, in short, constituted the uniforms of their trade. But it may at least be possible to suggest that for the skilled worker a noble, being roughly equal to a month's income, cannot have been encountered frequently if at all in the normal course of business and life. The poor naturally had less access to coins, whether of gold or silver, and the tendency of wealthier sections of society to retain or hoard cash exacerbated the problem for those lower down the economic chain.

Of the groups in society for whom England's new gold coinage will have had greater meaning the merchant class was the most likely. Trust engendered through possession of a purse full of gold nobles must have aided in the smooth concluding of a deal and in such a commercial environment nobles will have operated as a store of value or wealth, their survival today in good condition being testimony to a coin that did not always see the most active of lives. Evidence for a healthy demand is borne out by production of gold on a regular basis, some £0.5 million being struck in the first decade following the initial release, and through the preparation of a continuing series of indentures, the official documents authorising the manufacture of coinage at specific values, weights and finenesses. From this point on gold was to establish itself as a permanent feature of the circulating

Top. Gold nobles of Edward III were produced in large numbers from the mid-fourteenth century (enlarged).

Above. The lower face value of half-nobles of Edward III provided greater flexibility within England's range of gold coins.

coinage for the next 550 years, without question assisting in the liquidity of the money supply especially when access to adequate stocks of silver was compromised.

If the noble's role is best understood in the context of trade and in the hands of the merchant class, its design might also be explained in that same world. On the obverse the king is placed in the centre of a ship strongly resembling a merchantman of the time. Although the oversized figure of the monarch lends the coin a comic aspect, the image could be seen as conveying the message of England's right to occupy a prominent place in the trading community of Europe, which the arrival of the coin itself was seeking to augment. That the figure of the king is brandishing a sword and carrying a shield, however, could equally be thought rather belligerent in tone and could relate to victory over the French fleet four years before. The reverse of the noble carried what has been referred to as the royal cross, adapted from French coins, and through an elaborate composition incorporates lions, fleur-de-lis and crowns. A Latin motto taken from scripture finds its first outing here, the extract from Luke 4, 30, 'Jesus passing through the midst of them went His way', going on to become a familiar feature of the coin. Whatever the true message of its obverse, the trust fostered through an unchanging type spoke in favour of leaving the design largely unaltered for more than a century of production.

Golden angels

England's gold coinage settled into a familiar pattern of issues, consisting of the noble, alongside its half and quarter, until the mid-fifteenth century when the noble was revalued in 1464 to 8s 4d under Edward IV (1461-83). An abiding feature of the English coinage system, in contrast to some Continental practice, was its reputation for good standards of fineness and sound weight. The term sterling itself derived from a word meaning fixed or stable and, until the misadventure perpetrated by Henry VIII in the mid-sixteenth century, debasement had been avoided in favour of revaluations in response to increases in the price of precious metals. It had been happening in relation to the silver penny through a decline in weight from the thirteenth century and the enhancement of the face value of the noble was just such a readjustment, directed at maintaining supplies of gold by offering a price consistent with the market.

The difficulty was that the enhancement of 1464 had robbed the currency of the well-established and popular half-a-mark or third-of-a-pound denomination. As a solution, within a year a new coin was authorised, the angel, to be valued at the old rate of 6s 8d and like the noble it was to become an enduring feature of England's coinage, attracting over time a deep affection. But the changes did not stop there. Half-angels were introduced and a ryal, or rose noble, of ten shillings came in as well, accompanied by a half-ryal at five shillings and a quarter-ryal at 2s 6d. Within a couple of years the English gold coinage had become decidedly more complicated, authorisation being granted through indentures for no less than eight new coins. It might be questioned whether there was an actual need for such a variety of gold within the limited range of values, five shillings, 6s 8d and 8s 4d, but the situation settled down during the second half of Edward IV's reign, 1471-83, with angels and their halves being issued in larger numbers and coming to dominate output for the next 50 years. The changes of the 1460s provided England with a gold coinage of increasing sophistication, furnishing at the higher end of the denominational range the needs of the monied classes, with provision lower down being satisfied typically by half-angels and quarter-ryals. Wages had certainly advanced over the previous century but even the smallest gold coin would have represented a week's income for the skilled craftsman.

Essentially the design of the ryal was an adaptation of the noble but the angel was a different matter. Archangel St Michael is depicted standing over a writhing dragon into which he is thrusting a lance, a scene of some pictorial complexity compared to designs that had gone before and is certainly shorn of the naïvety of the noble. It is, indeed, notable that while silver coins continued to be the preserve of crosses, pellets and heavy inscriptional outer borders, the gold coinage in its first 120 years had taken on a much more expressive and elaborate visual language. By the time Richard III (1483-85) came to the throne gold had been part of England's currency for almost 140 years and over that time production, including coins struck at the English mint in Calais, amounted to just shy of £4.9 million. Output cannot be said to have been consistent year on year but by the last 25 years of the fifteenth century there was in operation a well-established and functional coinage of gold, sufficiently varied in its denominational range to match that of other European states.

Development of the currency had been responding to economic requirements but at the same time England had been riven by civil war during the second half of the fifteenth century. Yorkist and Lancastrian forces had divided the country and defined its political landscape; including wars with France, it is difficult to find a decade of genuine peace. Richard III's troubled reign famously provided William Shakespeare, writing more than 100 years later, with the most colourful of source material but it is no exaggeration to think of the politics of the age as bloodthirsty. To be a successful monarch required a strength of character and will which would by no means have been out of place in the pages of Machiavelli, himself a writer of the late fifteenth and early sixteenth centuries.

Within this setting of turmoil and conflict the currency systems of Europe were adapting to the demands placed upon them and accommodating new opportunities. Coinages had developed over the last two centuries to embrace a range of silver and gold denominations satisfying the needs of domestic circulation and cross-border trade. Towards the end of the fifteenth century a dramatic change, however, was about to make its presence felt as a result of ships venturing further afield and unlocking more of the world's natural resources. The wealthier of western European countries had already found a state-sponsored use for precious metals in the form of currency but through the increased supplies of bullion the means would exist to make bolder and more ostentatious statements through larger and more impressive coinages.

Above. A painting from the fifteenth century of Edward III in robes connected with the Order of the Garter, the order of chivalry which he founded. During his reign, through the introduction of the noble, a gold coinage was established on a firm footing.

Below. Angels, with their familiar face value of 6s 8d, became a regular feature of the English coinage from the mid-fifteenth century (enlarged).

Establishing the Tudor sovereign

The first sovereign

Richard III was defeated by Henry VII (1485-1509) at Bosworth in 1485 but if the new king were to be successful, in line with the spirit of the age, he would need to be shrewd and ruthless in equal measure. Internationally in the 15 years following his accession there was ferment. France under Charles VIII invaded Italy, conflicts flared up within states and monarchs, like Henry himself, were coming to power seeking to stake their own claim or make their own mark within Europe. For several years into his reign, to improve his tenuous claim to the throne, Henry had to deal with rebellion and conspiracies, a set of circumstances that can have done nothing to calm his naturally insecure nature. His marriage to Elizabeth of York, daughter of Edward IV, helped shore up his position by bringing together the houses of York and Lancaster and, while the decades of hostility were by no means immediately brought to an end, his suppression of dissent and his marriage alliance laid the foundations for a more united future.

Having a sound fiscal basis from which to govern was central to Henry's achievements and by actively pursuing the many sources of royal revenue with efficiency and determination, whether through enforcing fines or gathering fees, he gradually secured for the English crown a respectable level of financial security. As a character he is criticised as parsimonious to a degree that hindered England's development but there is evidence of his willingness to deploy resources when he could see a material benefit in doing so. The coinage fits into such a view of his character and reign, a means at his disposal to be used to meet a quite specific end, and one of the ways in which he demonstrated the point was through the first gold sovereign.

On 28 October 1489 Henry gave authority for the production of a new gold coin of 20 shillings in value, 15.55 grammes (240 grains) in weight and made from the traditional fine-gold standard established under Edward III. It was, by a distance, the largest coin yet issued in England. Sometimes coins acquire their names through usage, through the nicknames familiarity bestows upon them, but in this instance pretty well all the elements were drawn together at the start. It was by decree to be called a sovereign, amongst the most personal of names Henry could have chosen, suggesting a close association with the monarch himself. Indeed, the reform of the coinage more generally was an element of his own authority he was unwilling to see diluted or offered up to Parliament, and the monarchy, even into the early twenty-first century, has retained such prerogative powers.

In looking to establish the identity of his reign he naturally drew inspiration from the activities of his European contemporaries. With respect to the gold coinage, it has been suggested the example of the réal d'or of Emperor Maximilian (1486-1519) produced in 1487 for use in Flanders, Gelderland and Holland was the model Henry followed in determining to mint his gold sovereign. There were, however, other candidates, one of these being the series of gold coins issued by Enrique IV (1454-74) of Castile. It was an established coinage of a powerful European state, including coins of two, five, ten, 20 and 50 enriques, whereas the

Above. Portrait of Henry VII by an unknown Dutch artist from the early sixteenth century, about the same time as realistic portraits were first used on his silver coins.

Facing page. Reverse of Henry VII's gold sovereign of 1489 (enlarged).

réal d'or was a good deal more obscure and would have required a close knowledge of developments in the Low Countries. What may be significant in understanding Henry's mind at the time is that in March 1489 he concluded the Treaty of Medina del Campo with Ferdinand and Isabella whereby his infant son, Arthur, would marry the Spanish princess, Katherine. The Treaty positioned Henry's new dynasty well amongst the powerful states of Europe but it also suggests, in the year the first sovereign was authorised, his attention could well have been directed south rather than east. It is, however, probably more germane for there to be an understanding of the context in which the decision was made to issue the coin rather than knowing which specific model carried greater weight in his mind on the day.

Five types of sovereign from Henry's reign have survived and although not dated it is possible through the presence of mintmarks and an analysis of stylistic progression to establish an order of production. It is generally accepted that the first type to be struck is now known from a single specimen in the British Museum. Taking this piece as the one through which Henry's intentions were first expressed, it is a thoroughly arresting declaration. The enthroned portrait lends the coin grandeur, suggesting at once majesty and power trained on the person of the monarch. But the spectacle was further enhanced through the decision to depict Henry wearing a closed-arch crown, a conscious statement of imperial ambition.

A seated portrait and closed crown were key features but they had appeared on the English coinage prior to October 1489. In the spring of the same year a design showing the king enthroned had its first outing on silver pennies, a type that went on to become the standard penny design for the next 50 years. Likewise, the closed-arch crown is encountered initially on groats early in 1488 and in employing the device on the silver coinage Henry might be seen as projecting its symbolic meaning to a domestic audience as opposed to the more internationally connected users of gold. But in relation to his new sovereign, the importance of this particular type of crown was driven home more strongly still by positioning it prominently above the shield of the Royal Arms on the coin's reverse. Another important

aspect of the design is the enveloping double-rose which links and frames all the other elements. It was to become a defining Tudor symbol, marking the union of the warring houses of Lancaster and York, and here through its scale and clarity of execution helps create a singularly impressive design. Depth of engraving is conveyed through shading in the form of parallel lines defining the petals, achieving that holy grail of emblematic design in being highly stylised yet subtly natural.

Similar coins being issued elsewhere in Europe at about the same time, displaying skilfully engraved enthroned portraits, offers some explanation for Henry's decision to strike the first sovereign but it does not explain the choice of October 1489. The marriage treaty of March earlier that year secured dynastic succession for Henry's eldest son and linked England closely to Spain. In the wake of the treaty perhaps the new gold coin, with its obvious international profile, was a statement to other European powers, pointing to the opulence and wealth of Henry's court. An alternative, and more domestic-centred, explanation could be that Henry wanted the coin to be available for distribution on the occasion of naming his son Arthur as Prince of Wales in late November 1489, only a month after authorisation had been granted.

It clearly existed in a world of symbolism but it was money and being valued at 20 shillings it occupies the hugely important position of being England's first pound coin. A system of currency in which there were 12 pennies to a shilling and 20 shillings in a pound had been in place since late Anglo-Saxon times. Account entries in Domesday Book make reference to pounds, shillings and pence but it was to be another 400 years before any Englishman would have the opportunity to handle a single item of currency valued at one pound. It was under Henry, as well, that the other central element of the centuries-old system found a material expression from *c.* 1504 through the silver shilling, or testoon. The advent of the gold sovereign signifies the beginning of a gradual shift, which was to evolve further over the course of the sixteenth century, away from the mark of 13s 4d as a unit of account towards a coinage defined much more by the pound, its multiples and its fractions.

Above. Drawing of Henry VI on horseback from the fifteenth century showing the monarch wearing a closed-arch imperial crown.

Below. The commission of 28 October 1489 authorising the issue of the first gold sovereign.

Above. Sovereign-type penny of
Henry VII on which the king is
depicted enthroned.

Below. Silver groats of Henry VII
produced from 1488 combined the
medieval generic style of portrait
with a closed-arch crown.

Ongoing production

After October 1489, although sovereigns were not specifically referred to in
other indentures in the remaining 20 years of Henry's reign, there is clear
evidence through the sequencing of surviving specimens that they were
produced at regular intervals. Initial authorisation contained the instruction
for two sovereigns to be struck from each pound of gold produced and if
that direction had been followed to the letter 60,000 sovereigns could,
theoretically, have been manufactured. The question is whether the initial
stipulation was adhered to rigidly. How many dies, the tools originally used
in production, might have been employed can be deduced from coins now
extant, and on that basis it is likely that the quantity minted was a good deal
less than the notional maximum, with the lion's share of gold output being
directed in favour of the angel of 6s 8d, the workhorse of the gold coinage.
Large amounts of gold were produced from the mid 1490s, over £700,000,
and upwards of 60% of that output was concentrated into the last five years
of the reign. It has been estimated, again from die analysis of surviving
coins, that as many as two million angels could have been struck and if true
it would mean somewhat less than 40,000 sovereigns were made. Of the
remaining output of gold, small numbers of double-sovereigns, and even a
piece weighing in at 50 grammes, which was more than a triple-sovereign
and closer to the equivalent of ten angels, were made, combined with ryals
of ten shillings and limited quantities of half-angels.

If output of sovereigns was initially a fraction of overall gold
production, the proportion was probably a fair reflection of the coin's role.
Looked at in relation to the cost of goods at a time when a dozen eggs was
a halfpenny, a pound of butter a little over a penny and a sheep two shillings,
a 20-shilling coin would have been much less practical than any number of
smaller denominations. The merchant and professional classes of early
Tudor England had become accustomed to the angel, of which there were
reasonable quantities still in circulation from previous reigns, and then
along came a gold coin three times its value. Its limited use possibly resided
in the context of settling significant contracts for those engaged in trade,
especially across borders and, even more obviously than the larger silver
coins, gold of these proportions will have been the preserve of the rich. The
Royal Mint provides some point of reference for those earning a higher
income than is typically recorded for the building and farming sectors.
Across the range of its salaried officials, an example of someone moderately
well paid would be the Chief Engraver who between the mid-fifteenth and
mid-sixteenth centuries could have expected to receive £20 per annum.
Being in a position to secure other income from engraving work, and given
the more informal nature of how earnings were made up, his formally
recorded salary should be regarded as a baseline figure. But even so, with a
sovereign representing a good proportion of monthly income, the idea of
his handling one in the conduct of his affairs is questionable, pointing to
the quite limited ranks within society for whom the coin actually had
meaning. Such judgements, however, are fraught with difficulty, dependent
as they are not just on the level of income but also on the frequency with
which it was paid. There is evidence to suggest the Chief Engraver and his
colleagues received their salaries quarterly and in those circumstances the
denomination of coins disbursed may well have been at the higher end of
the scale.

Large and elaborately designed silver coins were also being produced
across Europe and like the spectacular gold pieces of the late fifteenth
century they functioned as money, if only as a way of representing or

holding a large amount of wealth. But in many instances the currency was being enlisted to help enhance the image of the monarchies concerned. These coins were the equivalent of a state demonstrating how wealthy and powerful it was through its ability to have such beautifully designed and intrinsically valuable objects produced. The same point was made through the manufacture of jewellery or impressive tableware decorating the lives of Europe's middle and upper classes but because a coin is itself a statement of a monarch's authority, expressing financial and economic control, large gold coins in particular conveyed an additional weight of meaning.

Giving and receiving gifts in connection with the customs of the royal court was well established, coronations, funerals, christenings or formal entries into a city providing opportunities for a monarch to make a gesture of munificence through the distribution of coinage or for high-ranking subjects to show their allegiance by offering a gift in return. For a monarch the use of coins in this context will often have involved gold and for Henry the angel, in particular, was the coin of choice when he was looking to reward a service or address a need. Illustrations survive in the records of the Privy Purse and what is apparent are the many instances in which Henry gave away amounts in sums relating to multiples of 6s 8d, the face value of an angel or half a mark. Given his fondness for the coin and his interest in modernisation it is not surprising to see its design undergoing something of a radical shift. Between 1493-95 out went the feathery medieval figure of St Michael and in came the more human Renaissance-style treatment of the dragon-slaying myth.

But the size, status and design of his new gold sovereign presented Henry with other options. In May 1502 the Treasurer of the Chamber, John Heron, recorded the gift of ten sovereigns to the Hungarian Ambassador, over and above an additional cash sum, and on another occasion a presentation of six sovereigns was made to a different representative from the same country. Separation of sovereigns here from the other monetary element reinforces the notion of the coin as special and distinct from normal currency. It can be no idle speculation to suggest that many other presentations went unrecorded in which the new gold coin would have played a role outside its function as money. The glimpsed record of such non-monetary uses is part of the aura that attaches to the gold sovereign, placing it in the personal setting of royal favour. Moreover, if the 20-shilling piece performed a marginal role in circulation there can be little if any doubt that double-sovereigns of Henry VII, having no presence in the record of coins officially authorised, were solely intended for purposes other than exchange.

Sovereign design over the 20 years from its initial release was adapted through five main types. Although they all conform to a basic arrangement of enthroned portrait on the obverse and rose-framed shield of the Royal Arms on the reverse, changes were made. Throughout the robes remain opulent, gathering in generous folds around the king's feet but, while the first sovereign had a plain background surrounding the throne, later ones became more elaborately decorated. The double-rose ripples across the surface of all sovereigns of the period but a particularly significant change from the initial striking was the removal of the immense closed-arch crown on the four later types. With the issue of the third sovereign design in 1493 there was a marked improvement in the quality of engraving which coincided with the presence of Alexander of Bruchsal, brought over from the Continent, it is believed, expressly to raise the standards of design and

Above. Two angels, the top one of Richard III showing a medieval-style treatment, while the lower one, of Henry VII, reveals an updated image of St Michael wearing armour.

workmanship. Importing skilled engravers from Europe was to be an approach followed by other Tudor monarchs and with them came a more flamboyant style in contrast to an English tradition that could at times be described as modest. Revealing a greater sense of perspective, the throne is wider, the carving of its back more finely worked and it is adorned with the familiar Tudor symbols of a dragon and greyhound. The figure of the king is drawn with great sensitivity down to the form of the hands and the way in which they hold the sceptre and orb. It is the work of a highly skilled engraver and the fourth type is, if anything, even more remarkable with its simulation of linen-fold panelling at the base of the throne. For the final sovereign of the reign Bruchsal is thought still to have been on commission but he probably did not execute the work himself and the contrast is apparent. Although handsomely proportioned, incorporating a large portcullis beneath the king's feet, which referenced the Beaufort line in Henry's descent through his mother, the style returned to a more unassuming approach.

On one level, the events of 1489 were no great innovation for the currency. A coinage of gold had already been in place in England for more than a century and the idea of a pound as a unit of account dated back at least 500 years. Moreover, using coins in the ceremonial setting of court life could hardly be described as groundbreaking. But Henry VII can be said to have modernised the English coinage. The medieval character of the angel was swept away in favour of a Renaissance-inspired composition, and realistic portraiture, in place of a simple pictorial image of royal authority, made its first appearance on English silver coins from *c.* 1504, again as a result of assimilating the cultural influence of northern Italy. When Henry's thin careful features were seen on groats it must have been an extraordinary moment; the greater part of the population will never before have met with the likeness of a monarch. Subsequently the new style of portrait was to appear on shillings of 12d, the first issue of that fundamental value in the English currency system as a single silver coin. But it is the gold sovereign that crowns all the changes, the original 20-shilling coin, if for no other reason than for its sheer panache. By the end of his reign England had a coinage actually representing the building blocks of the duodecimal system of pounds, shillings and pence.

Stability and reform under Henry VIII

England was a much more secure and prosperous realm when Henry VIII (1509-47) ascended the throne. Output of gold, which offers some indication of the health of the economy, continued at the robust levels sustained over the last years of his father, the pattern of production being dominated by angels and half-angels. Indeed, the sense of continuity was so strong that Henry VII's likeness continued to gaze in profile from the silver coins of his son until the mid 1520s and the design of sovereigns likewise remained largely unchanged during the first half of his reign. The type and range of gold coins altered with a series of currency reforms in 1526 and there followed a period of stability until the disastrous but profitable debasement of the 1540s. By the beginning of the 1560s the coinage had been restored but the legacy of the mid-Tudor years cast a long shadow on England's currency and life for those using gold and silver was a good deal more complicated than it had been.

That a coin was not authorised to be made in an indenture was no indication, necessarily, it would not be minted and that a particular denomination might be recorded in an indenture was, equally, no guarantee it would definitely issue forth from the moneyers' hall in the Tower of London. Sovereigns provide a good illustration in that while ryals and angels were provided for in the first indenture of Henry VIII in 1509, there

ANNO · ÆTATIS · · SVÆ · XLIX

21

Above. The rare sovereign of Henry VIII, produced during the 1530s, displaying the sun and clouds mintmark.

Below. Gold trial plate of 1542. Precious metal plates of this type were used in the testing of gold and silver coins to ensure their composition was correct.

is no mention of England's largest gold coin. They were, nevertheless, produced in the following years but given the extremely small numbers to have survived output was almost certainly modest and the more functional angel, as previously, vastly eclipsed their continuing presence.

Stability of these early years was brought under increasing pressure by changes to the coinages of England's main trading partners, in particular the Low Countries and France. Bullion flowed without huge restraint through Europe and changes to the weight and fineness of one currency could exercise an impact on that of another. The establishment of more attractive rates for turning silver and gold into coin at mints on the Continent, therefore, soon influenced a realignment in England to prevent the export of its coinage and in 1526, under the authority of Cardinal Wolsey, the Lord Chancellor, denominational values were altered. Following an initial enhancement of the face value of sovereigns and angels, which left their weight and fineness unchanged and also involved the introduction of entirely new coins, a further uplift was required later in the year and additional gold coins were conjured up. After the dust had settled, the face value of a sovereign stood at 22s 6d, angels at 7s 6d and a gold crown of the double-rose, struck to the new standard of 22 carats (916 fine) and valued at five shillings, had been introduced. As in the 1460s with the revaluation of the noble, the loss of the denomination 6s 8d was not well received, a requirement addressed through the short-lived George noble produced to the traditional fine-gold standard. These reforms represented a historic moment for England's gold coinage because they ushered in the adoption of the new standard of fineness, 22 carats, or crown gold, which ran alongside that of fine gold for many years to come. Almost immediately the reduced standard took hold and for the next 20 years or so dominated output. Between 1526 and 1544 about £20,000 in fine gold was minted, while production in crown gold was some 20 times greater.

Provision for sovereigns was made in 1526 but actual production of the coin at its new rating had to wait for a small and puzzling mintage of the mid-1530s. The pieces in question carry the highly unusual mintmark of a sun breaking through the clouds, present on obverse and reverse, a device which is not known on any other coins of the reign. One explanation is that

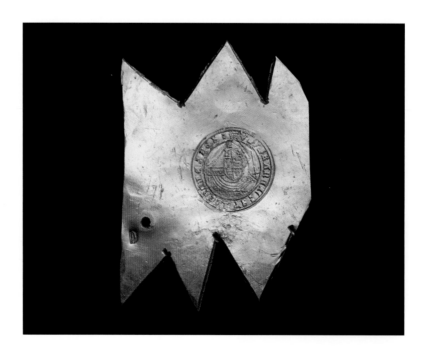

the strikings were ordered for the birth of Henry's son, the future Edward VI, reinforcing the role of the coin in connection with presentation and ceremony, but there remain doubts about the precise circumstances in which they were made.

On the eve of the debasement of the 1540s the gold sovereign could be described as connected to but somewhat separated from the regular business of coinage. From 1489 until 1526, in comparison to the production of angels, output of sovereigns was modest and, with the dominance of crown gold from the mid-1520s until the beginning of Henry's full-scale debasement in 1544, it looks as if sovereigns, again, played only a minor role as currency, their existence justified from time to time through ceremonial use. Increases in prices during the first half of the sixteenth century might have provided some help in making the coin more accessible but with wages remaining fairly static it could not be said that the net result of inflationary pressures would have influenced matters to any great extent, and the coin's rarity, in any case, defined its limited reach.

One way in which assertions about usage can be tested is through the record of coins deliberately buried in hoards or those casually lost. Very few hoards containing gold coins were deposited during the first half of the sixteenth century but 210 pieces were buried in Asthall, Oxfordshire, in the mid-1520s which included coins spanning the period 1470 to 1526. It was discovered in 2007 and predominantly included ryals, angels and half-angels but no sovereigns. That the greater part of the hoard was made up of recent issues of Henry VII and Henry VIII suggests it was fairly representative of coins then in circulation and the balance of contents is replicated in other hoards of the time. When Henry VIII's flagship the *Mary Rose* sank off Portsmouth harbour in July 1545, as well as heavy cannon, it was carrying hundreds of men who had as part of their personal possessions gold and silver coins. So far 28 gold coins have been brought up from the bottom of the Solent, the 19 angels possibly being carried as good-luck charms on account of their nautical designs. Although there were five newly-struck half-sovereigns, the absence of any sovereigns here and in other hoards is compelling evidence of how little they had filtered down into everyday life.

Above. The time capsule of mid-Tudor life revealed by the recovered contents of the *Mary Rose* includes gold angels of Henry VII.

Below. The Asthall hoard is one of the largest hoards of gold coins of the sixteenth century and provides evidence of the type of coins used in early Tudor England.

24

Debasement and renewal

Debasement of the coinage

The changes of the 1520s were the type of realignment the English coinage had been experiencing for centuries. Reform, however, of a considerably more politicised nature was enacted during the 1540s when Henry VIII instituted a systematic exploitation of the nation's currency for the profit of the crown. Temporary mints were opened to facilitate a debasement of the coinage and the culture connected with production changed from known systems of trust and reliability to a way of operating founded on deceit. The principle of the fraud was that new coins were made containing reduced amounts of precious metal, both in terms of weight and fineness, and issued at face values which did not reflect the changed metal content. Those presenting silver and gold for coining found themselves being offered higher rates and the seemingly more generous terms attracted large volumes of metal.

Financing war is a costly business in any age and when Henry found he was in conflict on two fronts, with Scotland as well as France, the Exchequer could not cope despite historically high levels of taxation being in place and money having already been extracted from the dissolution of the monasteries in the 1530s. One option would have been to constrain expenditure but there was little appetite for that and the coinage offered at least part of the solution. There had been an early experiment with debasement perpetrated in Ireland in 1536 and a further dalliance in 1542 but the main abuses began in earnest in 1544, continuing under Edward VI (1547-53) until 1551. Silver was more badly hit than gold with a savage reduction in fineness from the historic sterling standard of 11oz 2dwt (925 fine) ultimately to 3oz (250 fine). Fine gold was taken from 23 carats 3.5 grains (994.8 fine) in progressive steps to 20 carats (833 fine).

As far as sovereigns were concerned it was, strangely, something of a rebirth. The notion of the coin being minted in higher volumes than previously takes hold for the first time between 1544 and 1548, and half-sovereigns were struck in much greater numbers still. Moreover, since they were being produced at diminished standards they became slightly more approachable. A sovereign's face value was lowered from the awkward sum of 22s 6d back to its original 20 shillings but the weight was reduced from 15.55 grammes to 12.96 grammes and the fineness initially to 23 carats. Subsequent changes through the next few years resulted in a sovereign weighing 12.44 grammes of 20 carats, with a further weight reduction to 10.98 grammes in 1549 but at that point the fineness was adjusted back up to 22 carats.

It was a confused and chaotic jumble of coins that emerged. The years 1544-51 witnessed multiple changes in fineness, weight and value, with literally dozens of different types of coins being issued from no less than eight mints. Striking at York and Canterbury was resumed, and new mints were established at Bristol, Southwark, Dublin, Durham House on the Strand and even a separate operation was set up within the boundaries of the Tower itself. Multiple standards being released onto the market within

Above. The portrait of Edward VI by an unknown artist based on the painting by William Scrots, c. 1546, could have provided the inspiration for the bareheaded coinage effigy used on gold coins.

Facing page. The gold crown of Edward VI is remarkable for its sensitive depiction of the young king (enlarged).

the space of a few short years seems also to have stimulated experimentation in relation to design. Setting to one side all the negative implications of state-sponsored fraud, one of the blessings of this troubled time was the creation of a beautifully conceived series of coins. Durham House, especially, acquired for itself a reputation for an innovative or at least less than traditional output. A realistic portrait on English silver coins had been introduced within five years of the start of the sixteenth century and Henry VIII's own portrait was seen on silver groats from 1526. But a recognisable likeness on English gold coins does not arrive until the debased sovereigns of 1544, replacing the medieval-style generic depiction of monarchy and revealing the bearded king as a physically imposing man. The traditional design on the reverse of sovereigns, which for half a century had been a representation of the Royal Arms set within the decorative frame of an enlarged Tudor rose, now gave way to a full achievement of the Royal Arms complete with dragon and lion supporters.

A sense of renewal in the midst of chaos extended to new or revived denominations. Half-sovereigns had been authorised a decade earlier, originally at the rather awkward rate of 11s 3d, but specimens do not seem to have survived until the debased issues of 1544 when the more traditional value of ten shillings was applied. Gold ryals had carried that denomination since the mid-fifteenth century and they had continued to be provided for but had not been particularly popular in Tudor England. During the debasement years, however, half-sovereigns, more than sovereigns or the ubiquitous angel, were amongst the most commonly struck gold coins, with mintages sustained at a vigorous pace into the reign of Edward VI. A ten-shilling value was plainly regarded as more convenient than the 20-shilling sovereign and evidence of their popularity, beyond the sheer numbers made, is to be found in their presence in hoards of the second half of the sixteenth century. The Bisham Abbey hoard, buried about 1565-66 and recovered in 1878, contained 318 gold coins, over 50% of which were half-sovereigns, the majority, 134, being debased pieces of Henry VIII.

As the fraud was revealed the abuse of the coinage became progressively worse or, as Shakespeare would have Richard III say some 50 years later, 'but I am in so far in blood that sin will pluck on sin'. What was puzzling, however, was Henry's reticence to make further inroads into the precious-metal content of the gold coinage while still in need of additional funds. An explanation could lie in the much greater likelihood of those handling gold coins to weigh and test their fineness. On finding payments in debased gold being discounted, particularly on the international market, and the deception thereby exposed, merchants would have been much less inclined to have their gold converted into coins of a diminished standard. At a time in the late 1540s, therefore, when silver continued to be degraded the attacks on gold came to an end.

In the first two years of Edward VI's reign gold and silver coins were still being issued bearing designs carrying the name and often the likeness of his father but from then on there was a change. Half-sovereigns from his initial coinage show a crudely drawn plump-faced boy enveloped by heavily draped robes but from 1549 the portrait on sovereigns becomes more refined and the young king's attire more fashion-conscious. Holding an orb and sword, he is now wearing a finely decorated tunic, the sleeves gathered high on his upper arms and knee-length breeches, the shape of his legs mirroring the cabriole legs of the ornately engraved throne. Half-sovereigns of this second coinage, together with crowns and half-crowns, are even more exceptional. They carry a bareheaded profile, Edward's weak chin and parted lips framed by short-cropped hair combed forward to a high fringe. That he is shown without a crown is itself unusual and adds to the air of vulnerability conveyed through the slight features of an eleven-year-old boy. The extent to which those who engraved royal portraits for the coinage actually had access to their subject matter, or at least access to court paintings, is unclear but in this instance there are undeniable parallels with the well-known portrait by William Scrots dating from 1546. Although the direction in which Edward is facing on the coinage is flipped from the painting, as a die prepared by the engraver it would have faced in the same direction. Others of his coins bear more crudely drawn effigies but what is characteristic and memorable about Edward's gold coins are the crisply struck pieces which afford poignant access to the character of an English king as a young boy.

It is known, through entries in his own journal, that he took an active interest in the business of government and matters relating to the coinage naturally formed part of discussions. On 24 September 1551 he took the trouble to detail coinage designs he had approved, noting the use of Parliamentary robes and the chain of the Order of the Garter. After he had emerged from the shadow of some of his more overbearing protectors, it is tempting to imagine his taking the time to suggest a style of treatment prior to a final decision being made.

Realistic portraiture on English coins had its beginnings and early development on the Tudor coinage. Engravers had to learn the skill and in some instances, as was seen under Henry VII, the talents of overseas artists were imported to fill the gap. There is no question that from the first portrait of Henry VII on silver groats and testoons to those of Edward VI there was an increasing sophistication. They are by no means all classics and the requirements of everyday production took their toll on the vanity of the monarch but in the statement pieces, of which sovereigns and half-sovereigns are the most captivating examples, there are portraits that could rightly take their place alongside other highly regarded Tudor works of art.

Unlike some European countries, England had for hundreds of years resisted the temptation to debase its currency. There had been adjustments to the weight/value relationship of English gold coins in the previous two centuries and so, too, with English silver going back further still. Even when the new lower fineness of crown gold had been introduced in 1526, it had been enacted openly and with values assigned accordingly. At last, however, the potential income obtainable from defrauding the coinage proved too attractive, with some estimates putting the profit to the crown as high as £1.25 million. Other possibly unlooked for consequences of debasement included an upward pressure on prices brought about by those using the reduced-standard coins based on the amount of gold or silver they contained rather than at officially assigned rates. But of greater lasting impact, the decision to debase scarred the reputation of the English currency itself, engendering something of a crisis of confidence in sterling's reputation at home and abroad. What had been one of Europe's most trustworthy coinages was now tarnished with doubt and the sense of disgrace was to be felt for many years to come. During the debates surrounding the Great Recoinage of the 1690s, when questions were raised about reductions in weight and fineness, the ghost of debasement stirred and policy makers were urged to avoid the reputational damage to sterling visited upon the coinage in Tudor times.

Restoration and renewal

By 1551 the two-tier system of a fine-gold standard of over 23 carats and crown gold of 22 carats had been re-established and under the same indenture the striking of silver coins of restored alloy was also authorised. The practical problem of removing the debased silver from circulation proved more intractable and it was not until 1561, early in the reign of Elizabeth I (1558-1603), when the tainted issues of the 1540s and early 1550s were demonetised, that the currency returned to something approaching its

Above. While the standard of gold in sovereigns of Edward VI had been debased the quality of craftsmanship had in many instances been elevated.

pre-debasement standard. Elizabeth's tomb in Westminster Abbey lists the principal achievements of her reign, such as vanquishing the Spanish Armada, and amidst this select group of weighty accomplishments restoring the currency to its just value is recorded, a clear indication of its importance to the nation.

For sovereigns a new layer of complexity formed part of the settlement which was to continue on through to the end of the Tudor dynasty. From 1551 they were produced, albeit in modest numbers, in fine gold at a face value of 30 shillings, struck to the original weight of 15.55 grammes and bearing the traditional shield and double-rose design. At the same time a 22-carat sovereign was also sanctioned of 20 shillings, weighing 11.31 grammes and employing the crowned shield design with dragon and lion supporters first seen on the debased issues. Amongst the moves to modernise the coinage, which included use of dates in Roman numerals and the appearance of inscriptions rendered in Roman lettering, an air of medievalism remained through the continuing presence of the angel, now revalued as a ten-shilling coin, but struck in its traditional fine gold. From a practical point of view smaller value gold coins through crowns and half-crowns were provided for and before the end of Edward's reign in 1553 the more colourful end of the spectrum had also been explored. Piedfort-style double-weight sovereigns at the formidable bulk of 30.90 grammes, valued at 60 shillings, were struck, almost certainly destined for presentation. The immediate aftermath of debasement, therefore, saw the kind of realignment that could have been expected taking into account increases in the prices of precious metals and the need to establish a system with some expectation of longevity.

Established designs were retained but the spirit of innovation, so much a feature of the debasement years, continued. Edward is depicted on the 22-carat gold sovereigns and half-sovereigns crowned and half-length, wearing an elaborately decorated suit of armour, carrying an unsheathed sword in one hand and an orb in the other. It was an approach to royal portraiture by no means typical of English coins but was to be found on the Continent, in particular decorating the surfaces of large silver pieces. In terms of its use of royal iconography, it stood in marked contrast to the bareheaded Renaissance Prince of the earlier half-sovereigns.

In addition to the larger number of home-grown gold coins, the well-heeled merchant of the time would have expected to come across fairly large numbers of foreign coins. The fifteenth century had seen an influx into England of coins from other European countries and in the sixteenth century Henry VIII's activities in France had resulted in a rise in the profile of French gold coming to England. A good proportion will have found a new home in the melting pots of assayers and goldsmiths but much stayed in circulation. In the 1520s French crowns, as well as ducats and florins of northern Italy, were made legal tender and into the 1550s they remained part of the available stock of cash, one estimate suggesting that foreign gold made up as much as 9% of the total in circulation.

Hoards of the mid-sixteenth century confirm the views of contemporary commentators. Of the ten gold coins recovered on Holy Island, Northumberland, in 2012, from a hoard buried soon after 1562, five were Continental, including pieces from France, the Papal States and the Burgundian Netherlands. The much larger deposit at Bisham Abbey contained 18 foreign pieces, including Spanish, Portuguese and Venetian gold. In addition, records of gifts given to and by Elizabeth I to celebrate the advent of the New Year in 1565 show Sir Ambrose Cave, Chancellor of the Duchy of Lancaster, presenting the Queen with a black silk purse containing 'two portugues and two Doble soueraignes of xxx s the pece', the reference probably being to a Portuguese ten-ducat piece. Efforts under Elizabeth to drive such imports from circulation meant they were less readily encountered in the second half of the century in exchange or as gifts from her courtiers. On one level the regular users of high-value gold would have been familiar with a multiplicity of differing weights, values and alloys, emanating from several parts of Europe but the situation they confronted in post-debasement England was more bewildering than most.

Above. A Portuguese ten-ducat piece of the mid-sixteenth century.

Below. Elizabethan nest of troy weights of 1588 of a type that would become familiar in the regulation of the weight standards of the coinage.

In the midst of a greater range of gold coins the fine sovereigns of Edward VI were unmistakably of the same family as those of Henry VII 50 years before, a situation which obtained for the remainder of the century. During the mid-Tudor period, however, the English coinage underwent change of a different order – it became overtly feminine. Under Mary (1553-58) the only sovereigns struck were of 30 shillings in fine gold, every bit as elaborate and handsomely made as those of her forebears, but through the expected panoply of monarchy Mary is depicted with long hair cascading off and over her shoulders. The 15-shilling ryals produced during her reign also reveal that England had a queen. She is represented full-length, standing in a ship wearing a beautifully formed bodice, while on the silver coinage her depiction 'cooing and billing' with her Spanish husband Philip II became one of the best known designs of the later sixteenth century.

In a similar vein Elizabeth I projected the feminine side of Tudor majesty. Paintings of her in which she is placed at the centre of her court in procession or in isolated splendour gave the artists every facility to express her beauty and power. Within the small frame of a coin, however, the opportunity to make a grand statement was more tightly prescribed. For those coins produced in large numbers, particularly silver, comparatively little time will have been devoted to the completion of individual dies. There was, though, with the greater surface area and smaller mintages of higher value gold coins the opportunity to make a more significant artistic statement. Pieces of superior quality produced by Eloy Mestrell employing machinery within the Tower of London during the 1560s, as opposed to the traditional method of production using hand-held tools and a hammer, are outstanding, half-sovereigns and crowns being accorded the honour of becoming the first machine-struck English gold coins. But another impressive instance from towards the end of her reign is the 20-shilling crown-gold sovereign, the detail and finish of which suggest it was destined for a cabinet from the start. The crowned shield on the reverse is attractively proportioned, engraved with delicacy and crispness, surrounded by neatly spaced Roman lettering. Although stern and spinsterish in aspect, Elizabeth's portrait presents a glamorous figure, her smooth face emerging from a high ruffed collar and the dazzling facets of her robe. Over it all, like her half-sister, her hair flows in combed lines, merging with the heavily engraved detail. Both these Tudor queens brought to the English coinage a feminine elegance it would not see again until Britannia was refashioned under Charles II.

Output of gold under Elizabeth

A larger denominational structure provided options for the money-using public and coins were being called upon to work harder in circulation on account of advances in prices, wages and general economic activity. Given the increasingly monetised nature of the late-Tudor economy, however, and at the same time the reality of insufficient supplies of coins to meet the demands of growth, those needing to make payments had to look for other ways of conducting their business. A range of solutions was constantly being called upon to allow daily and weekly transactions to take place and, of those enlisted, credit was amongst the most important. It formed a key element of the world in which goods, labour and services were bought and sold, a substantial proportion of exchanges being carried out through some form of credit rather than by means of cash. The question of how much the ready supply and range of coinage influenced levels of credit or how the mechanism worked in the other direction is often difficult to disentangle but there is a clear sense in which coins and credit will have performed specific and critical functions. With respect to the coinage, outstanding

Top. A highly ornate gold ryal of Mary dated 1553 in Roman numerals.

Above. Machine-struck half-sovereign of Elizabeth I produced by Eloy Mestrell within the Tower of London in the 1560s.

Facing page. Portrait of Mary by Master John, 1544, prior to her accession to the throne.

ANNO DÑI   1 5 + 4

LADI MARI   DOVGHTER TO
THE MOST   VERTVOVS PRINC
KING HENRI   THE EIGHT

THE AGE OF   XXVIII YERES

31

balances, settled over weeks or months, would be cancelled off using higher value pieces; loans or payments for small amounts would involve gold or silver changing hands; and payment of rents, tithes or taxes would usually rely on cash. On a much larger scale, merchants would employ coins to pay for goods bought overseas or to seal a deal where paper currency, or bills of exchange, might not be acceptable.

Two families of gold coins had developed, with sovereigns of 30 shillings, angels and their respective fractions being made to the higher standard, and sovereigns of 20 shillings, accompanied by crowns of five shillings, with their associated halves, produced in 22-carat gold. Initially during the reign of Elizabeth very little crown gold was struck, and no 20-shilling sovereigns were made, but within four years the position had changed, with production of fine gold being almost entirely supplanted. The popularity of the crown-gold alloy had proven itself over the previous 40 years and half-sovereigns of ten shillings, or half-pounds as they have come to be called, look to have been issued in reasonable numbers.

Output then shifted in the 20 years from 1572 solely in the direction of fine gold, possibly motivated by a wish to return to pre-debasement standards, and plentiful amounts of gold continued to be processed, dominated in the 1570s by angels, half-angels and quarter-angels. Small numbers of sovereigns of 30 shillings, together with ryals of 15 shillings, were a feature of production from 1584 into the early 1590s, with a combined total of about 18,000 being made for the Earl of Leicester's campaign in the Netherlands during the mid-1580s. The balance of what was issuing forth from the Tower remained, nevertheless, firmly weighted towards the lower end of the denominational range, indicated by the production over the same period of some 100,000 angels. During the last ten years of Elizabeth's reign crown gold was again reinstated and as in the early years the amounts produced far outstripped the higher standard. While angels sustained a presence, no 30-shilling pieces were produced and the range of 22-carat coins, from the 20-shilling sovereign down to the half-crown of 2s 6d, formed a regular and sizeable part of gold output. Weights of gold and silver coins were adjusted in 1601, in response to changes in precious metal values, with the consequence that the crown-gold sovereign came down from 11.31 grammes to 11.14 grammes, while retaining its existing face value.

Total production over the course of Elizabeth's 44-year reign demonstrated there was not a great deal to choose between the two families of gold coins, £50,000 more in fine gold having been produced out of a total output of just over £800,000. What emerges, though, is a fine-gold coinage heavily dominated by angels, with the 30-shilling sovereign being struck at best sporadically, and a 22-carat gold coinage in which half-sovereigns of ten shillings played a consistently important role, backed by the steady issue of five-shilling crowns, while at the same time sovereigns of 20 shillings became integrated into regular production towards the end of the reign. Which of the two types of gold was more likely to be seen in domestic circulation is debatable but the balance may have rested in favour of the 22-carat standard since fine-gold coins had a greater chance of finding themselves being exported, as is suggested by the presence of angels and ryals in hoards of English coins found in the Low Countries.

Sovereigns in circulation

As during previous reigns, the double-rose and shield design was reserved for fine-gold sovereigns of Elizabeth I while for crown gold the shield of the Royal Arms was again employed but was now robbed of its supporters. For users, as well as weight and diameter, there was, therefore, a difference in design and as with any coinage familiarity will have been a worthwhile teacher. Those handling coins daily would have come to know that the debased Henry VIII half-sovereigns of 20 carats contained close to the same amount of gold as Elizabeth's 22-carat half-sovereigns, albeit of a slightly lower weight.

What could have caused more confusion was the inconsistency in naming coins of different values and indeed of the same value. At the lower end, the angel had become a ten-shilling coin in 1551, sitting alongside the half-sovereign of the same value which was itself also known as a new ryal and fairly consistently as a sovereign. The fine-gold sovereigns of Elizabeth struck in the 1580s were referred to as double-nobles, treble-sovereigns or great sovereigns, while the 20-shilling crown-gold sovereign was known as a sovereign or double-sovereign and has subsequently come to be known as a pound. Whether, or to what extent, the interchanging of terms was actually a problem is debatable since it will have depended on the context and the knowledge of the parties concerned in handling the coins. There is certainly evidence to suggest contemporaries knew exactly what they meant in assigning the name sovereign to a ten-shilling piece and valuing others in multiples on that basis.

Below. A half-sovereign of Elizabeth I which reveals the level of detail it was possible to incorporate into the relatively small frame of a gold coin (enlarged).

The appearance of coins in contemporary literature can provide some sense of how money was used and an indication of what the more popular denominations would have been. Writing towards the end of the sixteenth century, William Shakespeare was well placed to have a view about the currency of his age and at first glance the pages of his plays are hoard-like in their abundant reference to coins and money. Plots hinge on their presence and comedy is extracted from their double meanings. Nevertheless, while the term sovereign often occurs, he employs it in the context of monarchy or as an adjective rather than in relation to the coinage. There are sovereign kisses and sovereign lords, sovereign power and sovereign grace but, if the gold variety had become slightly more accessible amongst certain groups in society, it was conspicuous by its absence from Shakespeare's works. He was writing popular plays for a general audience and when he wanted to refer to an English gold coin it was the angel that frequently attracted his attention. Why, it could be asked, would he bother finding a role for a coin whose production was intermittent, whose name was transferable and whose circulation was limited?

Other literary sources of the time, indeed of the entire sixteenth century, are similarly unyielding. There is no shortage of reference to the word sovereign in the pages of essays, sermons, discourses, histories and plays but they are largely, as with Shakespeare, of a non-monetary nature and where the coin does appear, as in the rather dry setting of instructional books on teaching mathematics, buried amongst a host of other denominations, there is no insight into how the coins were used. Alternative terms, such as 20 or 30 shillings, do occur but they, too, are not plentiful and carry the uncertainty of whether an overall value was being mentioned or an actual piece of gold. The impression is of a coin, though splendid in form and bearing, living at the margins of everyday life and not at all anchored in the popular imagination.

Of witnesses to exchange and the handling of money the Goldsmiths' Company was better placed than most and when it commented upon the current state of the gold coinage in 1574 it saw angels, their halves and quarters, half-sovereigns, crowns and half-crowns being readily tendered, all with face values of ten shillings or less. Sovereigns of 20 and 30 shillings, as well as ryals of 15 shillings and old nobles, re-valued to 13s 4d, were known but were not normally used in payments. Other commentators were drawing the same conclusions a decade later, with higher value pieces being similarly excluded from lists of what was regarded as constituting currency in active circulation. In the will of Augustine Phillips, one of the partners who owned the Globe Theatre, Shakespeare was given a 30-shilling sovereign and the way in which it was recorded, as distinct from other cash, indicates a special status was being attached to the coin, consistent with its not being regarded as part of normal currency.

Reference to coins in wills of the deceased, as with Augustine Phillips, can often be a good indication of the sort of money held for use or as savings. They reveal, in a sense, what would be expected, that the poorer sections of society quite simply did not have coins at all and when money was listed only a small proportion of people had more than a few pounds. Inventories of the late sixteenth century show that while other gold coins – angels, ryals, as well as foreign pieces – could form part of the record of accumulated wealth, a sovereign was seldom if ever encountered.

Monitoring the activities of counterfeiters provides a good indication of what was readily passing in exchange since it is unlikely they would have wasted their time and gold on altering an existing coin or making one from scratch without there being the prospect of some profit. With that in mind, it appears half-sovereigns were what attracted their interest. There is evidence of shillings of Edward VI, which bore a strong resemblance to half-sovereigns, being gilded to pass as ten-shilling pieces and when gold coins were counterfeited, or when they were being clipped, it was half-sovereigns rather than the higher denominations that provided the focus of attention.

At the start of the sixteenth century the silver groat of fourpence, and its half, carried the burden of work in circulation. By the close of the century increases in prices had shifted the balance in favour of the shilling and sixpence. In relation to gold the coin that started out life as a 20-shilling piece weighing 15.55 grammes was still provided for in indentures but had increased its face value by 50% and at the same time the term sovereign was in some common usage being employed to describe a ten-shilling piece a third of the weight of the original coin. Coupled with these movements in weight and value, the cost of food between 1540 and 1600 more than trebled, industrial prices doubled and wages also advanced significantly, inflationary forces that should have worked in favour of making a coin of 20 shillings more useful. But even so, in buying the necessities of life it will have been a less than practical denomination. A pound of cheese at the end of the sixteenth century would have cost just under threepence and the same quantity of butter about fourpence while, for those seeking entertainment, to enjoy the relative comfort of a bench seat in one of the lower galleries at the Globe Theatre would have cost twopence. Where it came into its own was in the settling of a balance built up over weeks or months or in the purchase of more expensive items, such as livestock, a cow at the time costing about 50 shillings.

Above. Crowns and half-crowns of Elizabeth I formed a regular part of the output of gold coins in the second half of the sixteenth century.

The life of a gold coin, particularly of a higher value, in Tudor England was therefore likely to have been habitually sedentary. It would have involved lying around in bags, operating as material evidence of wealth or savings, and bearing witness to a natural reluctance to be given up when silver would suffice. An accumulated stock of gold might change hands in connection with major purchases, such as the buying and selling of property, and in those circumstances would be transferred wholesale, avoiding the need to be handled. The presence of worn gold coins in hoards is much less common than silver, as instanced by the Asthall hoard from the 1520s, the contents of which show no great indication of wear, even for the older coins represented from the fifteenth century. Smaller denomination gold, such as the crown or half-crown, will have experienced higher levels of exposure, aligned as they were to the value of silver, but it was the silver coinage itself which still bore the brunt of work in circulation. It made up a more significant proportion of the stock of coin in the sixteenth century, which will have strongly influenced patterns of use, and for the vast majority of the population access to any kind of gold coin was probably infrequent.

A carpenter in the 1490s who earned sixpence a day, which equated to an annual income of £5 or £6, a century later was possibly earning £10 annually and at approximately a month's income a coin of 20 shillings is unlikely to have formed part of the ebb and flow of his normal life. The Royal Mint engraver's salary of £20 in the early sixteenth century increased to £30 by the end of Elizabeth's reign and for him a half-sovereign of ten shillings, a crown of five shillings or a half-crown of 2s 6d will have represented more viable propositions. Higher up the income scale, once established as a popular playwright, Shakespeare would have inhabited a comfortable position in society, earning from Globe Theatre profits alone an estimated income of £40 a year. At that level he was in the same bracket as the gentleman class who could have lived well on such an income, and sovereigns of 20 shillings are likely to have been handled within that social group. Sovereigns of 30 shillings were another matter entirely, the limited numbers made, coupled with their high value, suggestive of a coin saved or given in special circumstances, such as Shakespeare's receipt of one on the death of his colleague. While salaries can provide some broad indication of who in society would have had the wherewithal to possess gold, the nature of employment could have influenced matters as well. Those operating in a commercial environment, such as wool merchants, would have placed upon them the requirement to deal with gold more frequently than a famous playwright and life in an urban centre probably brought with it greater exposure to the loftier denominations than in country districts. Regularity of encountering gold coins was no doubt therefore dependent on a range of forces, some but not all primarily determined by wealth.

Looked at from one perspective the greater variety of gold coins to evolve under the Tudor monarchs will have created more flexibility. On the other hand, the range could be viewed as complicated and congested, the gold sovereign providing an instructive case study with its different names, its variety of face values, weights and finenesses. The reality, though, was that people will have learned to cope and what seems to have been most in demand were gold coins between the values of five shillings and ten shillings, the weights of which varied over the course of the sixteenth century but tended to sit between 2.5 grammes and 6.5 grammes. Foreign coins that became popular in England fell within similar bounds and were valued in sterling accordingly.

Ceremonial use of sovereigns

In his *History of England, Scotland and Ireland*, published about 1587, Raphael Holinshed made the following observations: 'I have also beheld the sovereign of twenty shillings, and the piece of thirty shillings. I have heard likewise of pieces of forty shillings, three pounds, five pounds and ten pounds. But since there were few of them coined, and those only at the commandment of kings, yearly to bestow where their majesties thought good in lieu of new year's gifts and rewards: it is not requisite that I should remember them here amongst our current monies.' Holinshed's reference to presentation is illustrative of the alternative life the gold sovereign had from the start, played out in the grandeur of court when a statement or gesture was required. In Henry VIII's reign, sovereigns, ryals and crowns were employed on a regular basis as gifts. Early in 1551 under Edward VI a small number of sovereigns, angels and half-angels of pre-debasement weight and fineness was struck at the Southwark mint. The sovereigns were formally denominated 24 shillings, and would have been significantly undervalued for the purposes of circulation, but it is highly likely that the £2800 produced was intended for Edward's personal use. Angels were known to be a favourite of Henry VII at a time when they were at their most popular and Elizabeth, too, was very fond of them in the personal disbursements she made, possibly because they continued to be produced in fine gold.

Above. In their use of the Tudor double-rose fine-gold sovereigns of Elizabeth I bore a strong resemblance to the first sovereigns of Henry VII.

One of the most prominent of annual royal occasions when the exchanging of gifts was called for was held at New Year, a ceremony that had been taking place at least since the thirteenth century. Those recorded under Elizabeth indicate the giving of coins to the monarch was extensive and tended to be preferred by most earls, countesses and bishops, with those of the rank of baron giving a much greater variety of items, including jewellery and clothing. For the higher ranks of the nobility offering £10, £20 or £30 in cash every year was typical and expected. In return the Queen tended to give plate in the form of bowls, cups and even chandeliers, coins very rarely forming part of what she presented in return, at least at this ceremony. All manner of coins would change hands, taken from what was current at the time and drawing from the pool of foreign currency remaining in circulation. The angel had its place, an instance of which being Lord Burghley, the Lord High Treasurer, in 1582 presenting £20 in new angels; given his position, it is not surprising he might have had access to recently produced coins. While there were a number of ways of referring to higher value gold coins elsewhere, here an ordered pattern was in place whereby half-sovereigns were noted as such, or referred to as demi-sovereigns and valued at ten shillings, use of a sovereign meant a coin of 20 shillings and the term double-sovereign was assigned to 30-shilling pieces. Perhaps not as common as some other coins, sovereigns certainly featured. In 1559 the Countess of Worcester gave six double-sovereigns and on the same occasion Lord Richie offered 20 sovereigns contained in a red silk purse.

Over several years, however, the extent to which half-sovereigns formed an important part of the cash-giving element of the occasion becomes apparent, a reflection of the larger numbers being produced and the likelihood that those involved would wish to offer to the Queen newly-minted coins. Of the 169 individuals who presented gifts in 1571, 58 chose to make their offering solely in half-sovereigns, the total amounting to £723. The coin was particularly favoured by the clergy. Year after year the Archbishop of York tended to give £30 in half-sovereigns and the Archbishop of Canterbury £40. Detailed accounts of such exchanges through the second half of the sixteenth century offer a useful insight into the access this rank in society had to cash of a higher value and reveal coins acting out an important social function.

From unites to guineas

The end of an era

When James I (1603-25) came to the throne he united the crowns of England and Scotland. Within the first couple of years he had started to refashion himself as king of Great Britain and the coinage was one of the tools he used to cement his new status and to redefine royal identity through words and symbols. As king he had certain powers at his disposal which gave him the opportunity to change the iconography of the monarchy, and the coincidence of dates attaching to his enactments is almost certainly significant. Sovereigns of 20 shillings in crown gold weighing 11.14 grammes had been authorised by James two months after the start of the reign, the last that would be produced for some 200 years, and to the 22-carat suite of coins was added a half-sovereign, as well as a crown of five shillings and a half-crown of 2s 6d. The first indenture under James also provided for fine-gold angels, at the value of ten shillings, and their related halves and quarters, but none seem to have been issued during the first year and a half. All of which meant in effect the same range of coins as the last years of Elizabeth had been carried over, but the system was soon to be shaken up.

On 20 October 1604 James proclaimed himself king of Great Britain, France and Ireland. By an indenture of 11 November, three weeks later, the crown-gold 20-shilling coin was given a lower weight of 10.03 grammes and the new name of unite, an explicit reference to his achievement of bringing the crowns of England and Scotland together. James evidently judged sovereign a redundant term when the possibility was made plain to him that the naming of coins could be enlisted to his cause. The politicisation of the denominational language carried on down to the five-shilling piece being referred to as a Britain crown and a new four-shilling coin as the thistle crown. Further alteration to the old terminology led to half-sovereigns of ten shillings being re-named double-crowns, the 30-shilling piece changing in July 1605 to a rose ryal and a spur ryal of 15 shillings being authorised.

Other outward signs of government attended to included, not least, the nation's flag. A new design, combining the crosses of St Andrew and St George, was introduced from April 1606 but options were being developed from as early as 1604. In its essential design, if not its detail, what was approved at the time remains in use over 400 years later. James, in addition, altered his titles as monarch and the coinage became a ready vehicle for their display. Inscriptions on a number of his coins changed from making reference to the king of England, Scotland, France and Ireland to a monarch now presiding over the territory of Great Britain: IACOBUS D G MAG BRIT FRAN ET HIB REX, which translates as 'James by the Grace of God King of Great Britain, France and Ireland'. Demonstrating a little more subtlety, gold unites themselves from their first issue carried in Latin the quotation from Ezekiel 37, 22 'I will make them one nation'. A further aspect was to be explored through heraldry, involving the inclusion of Scotland's rampant lion, joining the well-established elements of England's three lions and the French fleur-de-lis. Taken together the changes represent one of the most thoroughgoing overhauls of state iconography yet seen. The idea of Britain as a political entity would take another century to resolve properly, but the deliberate and coordinated actions of James I were powerful statements of intent and one of their most prominent expressions was encountered on the king's new coins.

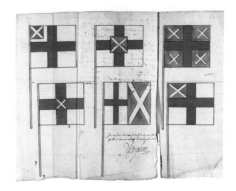

Top. Designs for a new Union Flag from 1604.

Above. Production of thistle crowns of James I arose from the currency reforms of 1604.

Facing page. Unites of James I replaced sovereigns as the principal gold coin but continued the tradition of a 20-shilling coin (enlarged).

Above. The laureate-style portrait of James I, used on 20-shilling gold laurels issued towards the end of his reign, had not previously been seen on English coins.

Below. A prominent piercing through angels of Charles I defined the coin's role in the ceremony and ritual of the Stuart court.

Unites and laurels

Sovereigns of 20 shillings were a casualty of the changes but as a unite the denomination survived and, indeed, thrived. Their production in increasingly large numbers reflected a general resurgence in the fortunes of gold which, having declined as a proportion of output compared to silver in the sixteenth century, now started to predominate.

While the gold sovereign was sidelined the tenacious angel kept going. Introduced by Edward IV in the 1460s, it had survived several revaluations and retained a place in the formal world of court life. After it had ceased to be part of normal currency, as a fine-gold coin it performed a role in the ritual of touching for the king's evil, to cure scrofula. Coins used for this purpose were pierced, threaded with a white ribbon and hung around the necks of recipients; the rarity today of unpierced specimens, particularly of Charles I, suggests the angel's function in life had by now become almost exclusively ceremonial. Another feature of the coinage to continue was the imposing Tudor rose which appeared, rather incongruously, through the first decade of a reigning Stuart king on the 30-shilling rose ryal. Output remained split between fine and 22-carat issues, but the proportion of fine-gold coins produced fell away quite noticeably in the early seventeenth century. A decline had already been evident towards the end of Elizabeth's reign but the trend accelerated such that by 1625 of the £4.3 million produced under James only about £31,000 of the higher standard was struck. The sheer practicality of a lower value and harder wearing alloy had eventually won through and that in some years, such as 1618, output of ryals and angels amounted to just a few hundred pounds is indicative of the largely ceremonial or political purpose the coins now performed.

Operating a currency system using both gold and silver, but without allowing either one a permanent position of precedence, meant emphasis could shift between the two at times quite dramatically. It required there to be adequate supplies in the first place, but if a more favourable price were offered to those bringing gold to be turned into coin than those presenting silver the economic reality would not be lost on the parties concerned. Under James changes to the weights and values of gold coins, as well as to the charges levied for having the coins made, operated in exactly this direction, resulting in larger quantities of gold being processed. The reforms of 1604 were not just a renaming exercise; the ratio between gold and silver had effectively been altered in favour of gold and other adjustments were authorised during the reign which made gold a more attractive proposition. An illustration of the impact can be seen in the output of gold in almost every year of James' reign being over £100,000, a substantial increase on what had been regularly produced under Elizabeth and in his last year as king more crown gold, in excess of £900,000, was produced than in the whole of Elizabeth's 44 years on the throne.

In appearance the 20-shilling unite followed the same design template of the late sixteenth century with a crowned profile portrait on the obverse and a crowned achievement of the Royal Arms on the reverse. The shape of the shield and the surrounding decoration were very similar to those of the late Tudor period and in choosing a half-length bust James looked not unlike Edward VI on his gold coins or several other contemporary European rulers. As the reign progressed the portrait on gold was revised to show a rugged-looking laureate bust to which common usage attached the name laurel. In style the portrait was much less weighed down with the trappings of monarchy but when his son ascended the throne as Charles I (1625-49) it was not an approach to which he found himself attracted, and instead there was an immediate return to the more formal Elizabethan design of high-ruffed collars.

Except for a brief few weeks in the summer of 1626, when the weights of gold and silver coins were decreased and then quickly restored, much remained the same between the two reigns. The 20-shilling gold coin had seen a reduction in its weight of almost 10% in 1604 when the unite was first issued and in 1623 its weight was lowered again to 9.10 grammes, which amounted to a further 9% decrease. These standards, though, were largely maintained under Charles from 1625, as was the tradition of striking fine-gold coins alongside the circulating standard of 22 carats. Production of the angel was indeed sustained until the early 1640s and although it continued to be authorised up to 1660, none seem to have been minted beyond the outbreak of Civil War in 1642. Their demise marked the end of fine gold, and with their passing a link with the original English gold coinage of the mid-fourteenth century had been severed, not to be restored until more recent times through the release of fine-gold bullion coins.

Fed by changes in the supply of precious metals, which was itself as much political as economic, the balance of output from the early 1630s shifted once more in favour of silver but during the 24 years of his reign £2.6 million of gold was struck for Charles I which, while much less than James over a similar number of years, was still historically high. Just as England could not escape being influenced by the flows of bullion through Europe, so the country was brought into the orbit of changes in technology within the minting industry. Experimentation with machinery had been explored by Eloy Mestrell in the 1560s and another attempt was initiated by the Frenchman Nicholas Briot. He had tried but failed to persuade the mint in Paris of the virtues of his techniques and in moving to England was allowed to set up his own operation in 1625 within the bounds of the Tower of London. The gold coins he produced, struck between 1631-32, conformed to the regular standard and included unites, double-crowns and crowns. They are delicately engraved and highly refined pieces, not only demonstrating Briot's technical mastery but also his ability as an artist to capture the subtle character of the king. It would be another 30 years before hammer-struck coins finally gave way to machinery but Briot's experiments made a lasting contribution and are evidence of the desire Charles had to improve the standard to which his coinage was made.

At a time of tension within the kingdom, it is not unexpected to see Charles, like many monarchs before him, turning to the coinage to make a political point. Output of the provincial mints set up to supply his currency needs during the Civil War, the Parliamentarians having seized the Tower early in 1642, provided him with just such an opportunity. Gold coins are known to have been struck at Shrewsbury, Oxford, Bristol, Truro, Exeter and Chester, as well as a couple of other locations as yet not definitively attributed, and in appearance they were on occasion attention-grabbing pieces. Up to that point unites of 20 shillings, double-crowns of ten shillings and crowns of five shillings had demonstrated an heraldic uniformity and then, starting with the triple-unite struck at the king's mint in Shrewsbury in 1642, an arresting design was devised based on a prominent inscription. Often rendered as three lines of a scrolling banner, the coins proclaim in Latin 'The religion of the Protestants, the laws of England, the liberty of Parliament', accompanied by the familiar biblical verse from Psalms 68, 1, 'Let God arise and let His enemies be scattered'. On the obverse Charles is depicted brandishing a sword in one hand and an olive branch in the other. The same impressively large gold coins were issued from Oxford, with the addition of unites and double-crowns following essentially the same design and silver of a similar type was produced again at Shrewsbury and Oxford

Above. Portrait of Charles I, in the style of Sir Anthony van Dyck, dating from the mid-1630s.

Above. The impressively large Oxford triple-unite of Charles I, 1643, was the vehicle for an unambiguous political message (enlarged).

Below. Commonwealth unites were of traditional weight and value, but the absence of a portrait gave the coins a highly distinctive appearance.

as well as Bristol. Elsewhere Sir Richard Vyvyan, Master at Truro and Exeter, struck gold and silver coins of conventional heraldic design, in keeping with the terms of his commission. Incorporating extracts from the Bible had been present since the first regular coinage of gold of the mid-fourteenth century but in its overtly didactic nature here Charles was going even further than his father James in explicitly politicising the coinage.

Having executed their king in January 1649 the leaders of the Commonwealth did not depart materially from the range, standard or names of gold coins established over the last 25 years. What did change significantly, however, was the design. How a republic chooses to represent itself on its coinage has long been problematic and the Commonwealth of England was no less challenged. The solution arrived at, with its shields on both sides, is one of the most heraldic of coinages and its simple use of English inscriptions resulted in plain and unencumbered designs in keeping with the tastes of the time. Bearing the paired shields of England and Ireland on one side, it was roundly lampooned by royalists as 'breeches for the Rump', a reference to the reduced numbers of those still serving as members of the House of Commons following internal dissent amongst Parliamentarians. A rather more conventional approach, though, was explored through yet another experiment into making coins using machinery, this time in the hands of the French engineer Peter Blondeau. He was allowed to set up a mint in Drury House and a small number of coins was produced between 1656-58, amongst them a 20-shilling piece known as a broad. Thomas Simon created a portrait of the Commonwealth leader, Oliver Cromwell, and in all its principal elements, wreathed profile bust cut short at the neck surrounded by an inscription defining the territories over which he presided, it was no different from the depiction of a Roman emperor. From the austere appearance of the early Commonwealth to an image of imperious self-esteem, these last issues before Cromwell's death in 1658 might be regarded as a revealing testament to how power can exert a strong influence over those who wield it.

The age of the machine

Unites and laurels had shown themselves to be worthwhile coinages and are accordingly well represented in the hoard record of the time. They made up the vast majority of the 113 English gold coins buried at Muckleford in Dorset towards the end of the 1630s and, amongst a larger number of lower value gold coins, they were well represented in the Tregwynt hoard, Pembrokeshire, dating from ten years later. During the first half of the seventeenth century the authorities had shown a fairly strong allegiance to the idea of a 20-shilling gold coin. Unites had been revalued in 1612 to 22 shillings but that adjustment was reversed in 1623 and, while the weight of the country's principal gold coin gradually declined, the logic of the unit of account being represented as a single coin prevailed. What lay ahead under the restored monarchy of Charles II (1660-85) modernised the coinage in how it was made and in how it looked but, to a much greater extent than had been the case previously, it found itself at the mercy of the market.

For the first two years of the new reign gold continued to be produced using the traditional technique of hand-held dies struck by a hammer and the same unites accompanied by familiar smaller denominations issued forth until October 1662. France had been using machinery to strike its coins since the mid-1640s and Charles' exposure in exile to that currency could have been influential in the decision finally being taken to adopt rolling mills and screw presses to make England's coinage. Historic hostility of the moneyers to developments in technology had been overcome and Blondeau found himself one of a group who in 1662 oversaw the introduction of machinery into the Tower. Production of new gold 20-shilling coins, struck only to the 22-carat standard, started towards the end of 1663 and from then on a date has consistently appeared on gold coins, having been a less reliable feature up to that point. Official sources were initially reluctant to give the coin a name but almost immediately it came to be known informally as the guinea on account of the west African origins of the gold shipped by the Africa Company from Guinea used in production. The presence on some gold coins of the small elephant badge of the company under the bust of Charles II, and indeed under the portraits of subsequent monarchs, was a visual acknowledgement of how the metal had been supplied. It was a lighter coin than its predecessor, from the indenture of 1670 being fixed at 8.38 grammes, and was joined by multiples of two-guineas and five-guineas, as well as by a half-guinea in 1669. A manifestly simpler structure for the gold coinage had been established which was to remain in place for the following 150 years.

The name of the coin now reflected the international nature of gold itself rather than being the expression of a domestic political ambition, and if what it was called was distinctive what it looked like was even more of a contrast with the immediate past. Being made using horse-drawn rolling mills the coinage blanks were flatter and more consistent, and being struck with the greater force supplied by the weighted arms of a screw press it became possible to impart a higher relief to the designs. It was now easier to make coins thicker which opened up a wider range of possibilities in configuring the edge with milling or lettering. Inscriptions on the edge of five-guinea pieces included, alongside the regnal year, the words DECUS ET TUTAMEN, meaning 'an ornament and a safeguard'. They had been suggested by the diarist John Evelyn but he was ultimately taking his inspiration from the *Aeneid* by the Roman poet Virgil. The words defined their purpose in being decorative in and of themselves while also acting as a deterrent to the clipping of gold from the edge of coins. Traditions sustain themselves across time on the British coinage, an instance of which is to be

Above. The gold 20-shilling broad of Oliver Cromwell, 1656, has a milled edge which later became a standard security feature of higher value coins.

Below. Guinea of Charles II, 1663, incorporating the elephant badge of the Africa Company below the bust of the king.

seen in the continued appearance of the same inscription on modern one pound coins from 1983. Given the limited circulation of five-guinea pieces the 'ornament' part of the inscription was probably of more relevance but the presence of milling on guineas and two-guinea pieces was another matter and must have aided in the fight against those seeking illegally to diminish the coinage through clipping, as well as in time also coming to be seen as protection against counterfeiting. Output of the machines has come to be known as the milled coinage, the term deriving from the use of rolling mills in the production process rather than, as is often mistakenly assumed, from the presence of milling on some of the new coins.

Below. Five-guinea piece of Charles II, 1668, showing a lettered edge which protected and decorated the coin (enlarged).

Thomas Simon created a sophisticated portrait of Charles II, which appeared on his Petition crown, but it was the work of John Roettiers, accomplished in its own right, that fulfilled the requirements of mass production under the new system. In appearance the gold coins of the late seventeenth century were fine-looking pieces, bearing for the most part cruciform arrangements of the Royal Arms and well executed effigies, a particular high point being the joint portrait of William and Mary (1689-94), the first time such a composition had been used on English gold coins, the double portrait of Philip and Mary of the mid-sixteenth century only finding a place on silver.

Guineas took on an increasingly visible role in commerce and industry, and as well as bankers choosing to base their reserves to a considerable extent on them, tax collectors came to prefer them to the flagging substance of the silver coinage. In the 40 years from the restoration of the monarchy to the end of the seventeenth century £8.3 million in gold was produced, twice the amount of the preceding 40 years. A healthy demand was evidently being met but gold had to contend with being priced in relation to silver and the balance of supply had forced up the exchange value of the guinea beyond the nominal rate assigned to the coin by government. Officially guineas circulated at 20 shillings but in practice they had changed hands at 21 shillings and 21s 6d within the first decade of being issued. Towards the end of the century the situation grew considerably more unstable, partly as a result of the financial pressures arising from being at war with France from 1689 but also because of the difficulties that started to become evident through the old hammered silver coins circulating alongside the machine-made full-weight pieces. Worn silver from former times, with its thinner profile, was subjected to clipping to an alarming degree and the value of gold in terms of these ravaged pieces rose, at one point in May 1695, to 30 shillings. The extensive, and expensive, recoinage that followed over the next few years, paid for by a tax on windows which remained in force until 1851, involved calling in all the hammered silver and issuing in its place coins produced on screw presses. A handsome coinage emerged that not only laid to rest the destabilising epidemic of clipping but also enabled the guinea to be reduced in value by stages ultimately in 1699 to 21s 6d, a rate at which it was to remain until it was permanently fixed in 1717 at 21 shillings.

There was, however, a problem lurking at the heart of the Great Recoinage of silver of the 1690s and in the operation of a bimetallic system it had an impact on gold. The reforms had retained the existing composition, weights and denominations of silver coins which left them undervalued and during the coming decades actions taken by government to solve the problem, such as encouraging silver to be offered for coining or altering the relative values between silver and gold, ultimately did not improve the situation. Those seeking a more lucrative market for their silver shipped it abroad, a situation the London merchant Simon Clement summed up by observing, 'the solid Wealth of the Kingdom is sinking into the Indian Seas'. As far as gold was concerned the position was, by contrast, largely positive with healthy amounts being turned into coin through the reign of William III (1694-1702) and that of the last Stuart monarch Queen Anne (1702-14). In an effort to bring the system into balance, Sir Isaac Newton, who was Master of the nation's mint at the time, recommended in 1717 fixing the guinea's face value at a maximum of 21 shillings. The recommendation was accepted and on that basis the guinea went on to become the principal British gold coin of the eighteenth century. But the further adjustments in favour of silver that were necessary never came and the measure had little if any impact on the amount of silver minted, leading to an imbalance between the two coinages for the next 100 years.

Above. A skilled engraver could have taken two weeks or more to prepare this guinea portrait punch of Charles II.

Guineas in the eighteenth century

With London growing in importance as a centre for international commerce and Britain more generally becoming wealthier, there was a ready market for gold to play a higher profile role. Portugal was importing the metal from South America, and Britain found it was able to absorb substantial inflows which were in turn reflected in a shifting balance of output, the contribution of silver coins by value representing a tiny proportion of what was put into circulation. Writing in 1730, John Conduitt, who was Newton's successor as Master, commented that, 'nine parts in ten, or more, of all payments in *England*, are now made in gold'.

What had been an extensive range of gold coins in the sixteenth century had given way gradually to a much simpler system based entirely on the guinea, its multiples and fractions, all made from the same 22-carat gold. It was the guinea itself, though, that dominated the scene, its half never proving as functional or popular. Efforts to have smaller gold coins take the place of larger silver denominations, and so ease the problem of supply, were not particularly successful. A quarter-guinea of 5s 3d was provided for in the indenture of 1718 under George I (1714-27) but was only struck in that year and in 1762, and while the third-guinea of seven shillings fared better, being issued for several years after 1797 at the urging of the Bank of England, it found itself fighting for survival, as did all gold in circulation, during a time of war with France at the turn of the century. The presence of foreign coins happily rubbing shoulders with the domestic output remained a feature of what was used as currency and will have complicated matters somewhat but not to the extent that would have caused undue confusion to the well-informed. Moidores from Portugal, valued at 27 shillings, were in particular strongly represented, especially following the Methuen trade treaty with Portugal of 1703. They are seen recorded alongside British and other overseas coins on handwritten tables pasted into pocket balances, a clear indication of how readily they would have been encountered and a reminder that the quantities of guineas being made were evidently not enough.

Above. Third-guineas and quarter-guineas of George III were issued to help alleviate the shortage of silver coins but never gained popularity.

Below left. Pocket balance used to weigh coins of all types and descriptions from whatever part of the world.

Below. The existence of individual weights for Portuguese coins demonstrates the extent to which foreign coins were used regularly in Britain in the eighteenth century.

Facing page. Five-guinea piece of William and Mary, one of the most handsome coins of the late seventeenth century (enlarged).

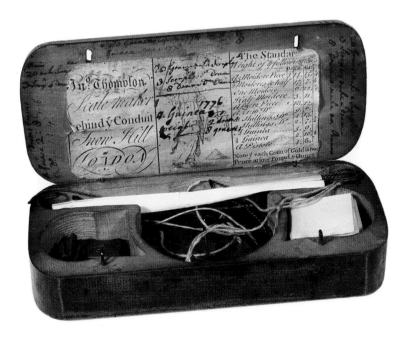

Above. Half-guineas of George II, like other British coins of the time, bore Royal Arms and titles reflecting the German possessions of the Hanoverian dynasty.

Below. Vigo five-guinea piece of Anne, 1703, struck to commemorate the seizure of a quantity of precious metal off the north coast of Spain.

Hammered gold from before 1663 and milled from after had circulated side by side well into the eighteenth century without anything like the crisis of clipping that afflicted silver in the 1690s, but by the 1730s there was a recognition the time had come to call in the old money. Gold from the reigns of James I and Charles I, issued 100 years earlier, remained in use and even pieces dating back to the sixteenth century were said to be current. Revenue officials and banks had long since refused to accept them prior to their being withdrawn during 1733-34 and once the recoinage was under way some 15,500lb of the coins found their way into the melting pot.

In the second half of the eighteenth century gold's dominance was mirrored by silver's decline. A century earlier £22.5 million of silver coin had been made, while in the eighteenth century the figure was less than £1 million, a level that had not been seen since the fifteenth century. In consequence a smaller number of silver coins had to work harder and those remaining became worn almost beyond recognition. By contrast, output of gold reached over £1 million in a single year in 1701, the first time that had happened, and during the last quarter of the century £47 million in gold coin was produced, a staggering amount compared with any prior period and more than double the previous 25 years. Perhaps as a function of the larger amounts being processed, the sources from which bullion was being drawn came to be increasingly centralised as the century advanced. There remained instances of supply being provided through the traditional seizure of treasure from rival countries, such as the publicly prominent action at Vigo off the north coast of Spain in 1702, a recognition of which appeared on gold and silver coins through the word VIGO. While the silver captured totalled 4500lb, the gold involved was the embarrassingly small amount of 7lb 8oz, contrasting sharply with the much larger sum acquired in the 1740s which resulted in the appearance of the word LIMA on certain gold and silver coins. But as such windfall contributions from privateering declined, and as the banking sector grew in influence, the supply of bullion came to reside more exclusively in the hands of the Bank of England.

Withdrawing hammered gold in the 1730s helped improve the condition of coins in circulation but such actions of practical regulation on the part of government had not yet become frequent or systematic. It was all very well for the circumstances to be provided in which coins could be made but with the increasing importance of gold to the economy the authorities could not allow it to be left thereafter unmanaged. By the 1770s gold and silver had worn substantially but in the balance between the two Adam Smith was correct in observing that 'the gold, that part of it at least which circulated in London and its neighbourhood, was in general less degraded below its standard weight than the greater part of silver'. Merchants and other traders were nonetheless finding it profitable to pick out heavier guineas and have them shipped abroad, increasing the proportion of light coins remaining. In addition, a rise in the price of gold through the 1760s became connected in the minds of officials to the defective condition of the coinage. Under pressure of such forces a recoinage was authorised and from 1773 worn gold was called in, the maximum allowance for weight loss being set at 4.5% after which a coin would only be taken as bullion. The highest rates of wear, over 7%, were recorded from the first withdrawals but even at that level the condition of guineas was still significantly better than shillings.

It was a demanding programme of work. During the four years of the recoinage up to 1777 approaching £20 million was produced, of which about £16.5 million came from deficient coin. But while the exercise represented a huge investment in rejuvenating the fabric of the currency on the part of government, the recoinage itself did not solve the problem of

light gold. To maintain the condition of coins in active circulation a Royal Proclamation was prepared in April 1776 directing that guineas worn below a certain level from the standard weight should be taken at their bullion value only. But because no long-term provision had been made for the regular withdrawal and renewal of the coinage, the old symptoms soon re-emerged. There were descriptions in 1786 of alarming increases in light gold coins, many arriving from America after the War of Independence, that caused bankers in London to refuse guineas below an acceptable weight. It would be another century, however, before a government-funded scheme of continual recoinage was introduced which provided a solution for the perennial problem. Nevertheless, what had become abundantly clear through the need to renew the gold coinage in the 1730s and again 40 years later was the way in which its use had been transformed from Tudor times. In contrast to its being an important although largely inactive store of wealth, gold was now fully engaged in the routine business of exchange.

Guineas and half-guineas of the recoinage carried the right-facing portrait of George III (1760-1820) on the obverse and the shield of the Royal Arms on the reverse. Over the course of his long reign several designs for guineas were devised, the best known being the spade guineas issued from 1787, so named on account of the shape of the shield chosen to frame the Royal Arms. As a series the gold coins of the time were not the most artistically accomplished and the extent, as well as the speed, of output from time to time compromised quality.

British currency in the late eighteenth century

The situation may not have been ideal but towards the end of the eighteenth century Britain's gold coinage was reasonably well maintained, certainly in contrast to silver which was so heavily worn hardly any vestige of design

Above. The spade guinea of George III became one of the best known coins of the late eighteenth century (enlarged).

Above. Spanish dollars countermarked with the bust of George III circulated readily in Britain in the late eighteenth century.

Facing page. The extent to which gold coins had been driven from circulation as a result of war with France led to satirical cartoons being published suggesting bankers might have been taken by surprise if they ever came across a guinea.

remained. Copper had become a more important part of the currency but its circulation consisted of a tired official coinage propped up from the 1780s by large quantities of privately manufactured tokens. Credit remained a key element of the economy, the shortages of cash extending periods allowed for payment and highlighting the importance of trust in how transactions were carried out. At the same time banknotes were being used more frequently, promoted by a strong Bank of England and a network of hundreds of private banks scattered throughout the country. A range of payment options therefore existed but in relation to the coinage the position was, ultimately, one of imbalance and when the impact of revolution in France came to be felt on the mainland of Britain the currency was in no fit state to stand up to the assault.

Wars have a habit of playing havoc with a country's currency. That between Britain and France, fought from the 1790s through to 1815, exacted a profound influence on many aspects of national life, not least the coinage. The financial crisis engendered by a failed invasion of disorganised French troops in February 1797 was massively out of proportion to the scale of the military threat but William Pitt's government had to respond to the panic of people rushing to withdraw their gold from banks. A series of interrelated measures was hastily drawn together which provided for one pound and two-pound banknotes, an emergency issue of countermarked Spanish dollars, a proper recoinage of copper, the striking of third-guineas and, importantly, restrictions being placed on the Bank of England's obligation to pay its notes in gold. The impact was immediate and lasting, shock waves from the crisis rippling through the next two decades of British history.

An increase in economic activity and employment was one of the positive consequences of war with France but the associated disruption drove guineas out of circulation. Britain, though, muddled through with additional temporary issues of silver and much greater reliance on banknotes than had ever been the case previously. *The Times* proclaimed some years after the commotion had abated that in the wake of Bank restriction had come 'a miserable debased currency, the disgrace of our country in the eyes of all foreigners', and was concerned that even the religious education of children had suffered. A whole generation, the newspaper lamented, would probably fail to understand the parable of tribute money because 'the greater part of the counters which pass among us for money have either no image or superscription'. Given the context in which they were and were not being used, it is in some ways not surprising that the last guineas to be struck in 1813 turned out to be in connection with war against France, the so-called military guineas, produced expressly for allied forces on the Continent advancing against Napoleon. By the time Wellington returned from his success on the battlefield of Waterloo reform of the currency was long overdue and the prospect of stability through peace provided an opportunity for a fresh start.

The gold standard

A new hope

During the 200 years after James I chose to abandon the gold sovereign, in one form or another a coin continued to be issued that broadly speaking represented the unit of account. Through a series of adjustments it gradually lost about a quarter of its weight, its diameter reduced from 40mm to 25mm and its fineness was confirmed at 22-carat gold. Designs shifted with the mood of the age but a depiction of the monarch and a treatment of the Royal Arms tended to remain the favoured solution. Of greater impact on appearance was the introduction of machinery, reflected in a modern-looking coin, thicker and more regular in dimensions. The most significant change, though, came with the extent to which a gold coin of about 20 shillings was made and used. Annual output of gold increased from an average of less than £15,000 in the last decade of Elizabeth I's reign to exceeding £2 million on a regular basis by the end of the eighteenth century, clearly demonstrating the strong demand that existed for gold coins which in turn exercised a powerful influence over those who were called up to reform the British currency after Waterloo.

As war against France had continued, and as the government had devised more and more imaginative ways of financing it, so the British currency was scrutinised in much greater detail. Instead of being a backwater of political debate, the quantity of notes in circulation and how the coinage might be reformed became live issues and the theme for a group of writers who increasingly turned their attention to economic questions. An extended treatise on the subject of how the coinage should be reformed had been published in 1805 by Charles Jenkinson, the first Earl of Liverpool, and many of his ideas found their way into the legislation his son Robert Jenkinson, the Prime Minister, introduced in the summer of 1816. The Royal Mint had, at the same time, found itself a new purpose-built home on Tower Hill and steam-powered machinery designed by Matthew Boulton and James Watt for use in Boulton's mint at Soho, Birmingham, had been installed.

After the best part of a century of operating an unofficial gold standard, Britain now finally acknowledged the reality on the ground with formal legislation. To support the settlement new coinages of gold and silver were introduced, the reforms amounting to a systematic overhaul of the existing arrangements. From now on the value of Britain's currency would be tied to the value of gold but there was initially some debate about whether the guinea would be retained or a new coin should be introduced. The Royal Mint's Master, William Wellesley Pole, supported the guinea on the grounds that it was very widely accepted and recoining a potentially large number would be inconvenient. But however much the coin had become entrenched in the nation's affections, use of one pound notes during the Napoleonic Wars had enhanced familiarity with the 20-shilling denomination over the 21 shillings of the guinea and virtually every speaker in the House of Commons during the second reading of the Coinage Bill in the summer of 1816 made a point of expressing support for the introduction of a coin denominated 20 shillings. Government was ultimately persuaded and in musing on the prospect Pole contented himself with the thought that if the appearance of the new coin could be sufficiently distinct from the old there might be no confusion from their circulating alongside one another.

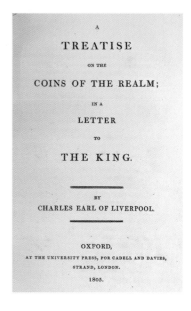

A

TREATISE

ON THE

COINS OF THE REALM;

IN A

LETTER

TO

THE KING.

BY

CHARLES EARL OF LIVERPOOL.

OXFORD,

AT THE UNIVERSITY PRESS, FOR CADELL AND DAVIES,
STRAND, LONDON.

1805.

Above. The title page of Lord Liverpool's published letter to George III which expounded his ideas on the future of the British coinage.

Facing page. St George and the dragon reverse of a George III sovereign of 1817 (enlarged).

Details of what Pole was required to do were drawn together, as they had been for hundreds of years, in an indenture, in this instance dated February 1817. Its significance lies not just in the role it played in defining the operation of the gold standard but in its being the last such contract in relation to the coinage. Directions governing which coins were to be produced and to what standard were from the mid-nineteenth century provided by instructions from the Treasury and confirmed, as required, through Royal Proclamations or Acts of Parliament. Physical embodiment of the gold standard was finally determined as a coin weighing 7.988 grammes and abundant evidence, especially from the second half of the eighteenth century, would have provided government with the reassurance it was pitching the weight/value relationship at the right level.

As a unit of account the pound had certainly drifted down the social hierarchy from early Stuart times. The Royal Mint's own record of salaries shows that the Weigher and Teller, who occupied a fairly senior position in the hierarchy, would have seen his income increase from £33 at the beginning of the seventeenth century to £200 by 1817 and he would thereby have become much more closely acquainted with higher value gold coins as the centuries advanced. But as in former times, such headline figures need to be treated with caution because formal salaries were only a part of the picture. In 1732 an account survives of how the income of the Headmaster of Eton College was made up. 'The Master of Eaton school has one allocation of £50 per ann., and another of £12; in all £62 per ann. Besides this, he has commons of all kinds, bread, beer, and easements of all sorts without paying a single farthing. This cannot easily be computed at less than 10s. per week.' Further details are provided of other sources of funds arising from rent and fees but the overall amount is, in one sense, less important than the light it sheds on a network of incomes, as opposed to one single salary.

Perquisites had by no means disappeared by the beginning of the nineteenth century but they probably became a less significant aspect of overall income as the century advanced. Clerks working for the East India Company were amongst the best paid of the growing numbers of that sector employed in government and banking. At the lower end they would have earned roughly £60 in 1815, one with much more experience over £500 and their department heads at least £1200. About a decade later a junior clerk at Coutts bank would have expected a salary of just over £100 and there was a large group of clerks across a range of organisations whose income in the 1820s ranged from £50 to £150 a year depending on age and experience. For those on an annual salary in the region of £500, firmly embedded in the ranks of the middle class, whose monthly income was over £40, the sight of a 20-shilling coin should have been fairly common and for their more highly paid colleagues, who were earning in a month what a senior government official would have hoped to receive in a year at the end of Elizabeth's reign, sovereigns amounted to a modest sum. Clerks on £100 a year will have seen matters a little differently but with a coin of 20 shillings for them being half a week's pay its use would perhaps not have been infrequent.

Amidst the expectation of there being a gold coin of 20 shillings there was, as Pole had discerned, the need for a contrast with the former guinea and this extended to what the new coin was to be called. As officials embarked upon the process of reform, it is unlikely the name sovereign sat at the top of any list of options. When Samuel Johnson was preparing his dictionary of the English language in the 1750s he quite rightly found a place for the guinea, defined as 'a gold coin valued at one and twenty shillings' but reference to a gold coin by the name of sovereign is absent. Its place in the popular imagination of the eighteenth century, as expressed through the literature of the age, is also difficult to locate. While authors like Henry Fielding were fond of phrases such as sovereign contempt or sovereign remedies, or through the word's association with monarchy, there is little if anything connecting it with currency. By the end of the eighteenth century, and indeed for many years before, knowledge of the gold sovereign had passed from living memory. But the name seems to have been rediscovered by antiquarians interested in the study of numismatics and the currency reforms following the war with France provided an opportunity for a revival.

That the academic interests of a very small group could find their researches turned into the provisions of coinage legislation is not, given the personalities involved, as fanciful a proposition as it might seem. William Wellesley Pole, an elder brother of the Duke of Wellington, was well connected with the community of those engaged with the history and aesthetic qualities of the coinage. Sir Joseph Banks and his sister Sarah Sophia Banks, the respected collector whose interests included coinage, were friends of his and there were others sympathetic to the cause of revitalising the fortunes of Britain's currency who helped Pole transform the coinage in the last years of George III's reign.

Above. The Royal Mint was led by William Wellesley Pole in the years following Waterloo and he oversaw significant changes to the coinage.

Designing the gold sovereign

Pole was a member of a remarkable Irish family which in a single generation had given Britain a formidable statesman in Lord Wellesley, a skilled diplomat in Lord Cowley, its finest military leader in the Duke of Wellington, and threw in a Bishop of Durham for good measure. He was not a man of parts in quite the same way as his more famous brothers, but he had an interest in art belied by the image of him as overbearing and self-regarding passed down in the pages of political histories and satires. There is no question he reveals himself at times as arrogant, but Pole had a vision and he promoted it in innovative ways which sometimes seem unnervingly modern. He would exhort his colleagues to believe the coinage should stand unrivalled for the excellence of its design and, far from being empty rhetoric, he devoted energy and passion to realising his ambitions.

The principal means through which he was able to execute his vision walked into his life in the first few months of 1816 in the shape of the Italian gem engraver Benedetto Pistrucci. An artist of some repute in his field, he came to Britain in the summer of 1815 and almost immediately attracted patrons and supporters. Apart from a few collectors and connoisseurs he was, though, initially unknown and yet within a year he was given the most prestigious job any numismatic artist could wish to have – preparing the coinage portrait of a reigning monarch and, in addition, the reverse of the nation's principal gold coin. With great talent can often come controversy and throughout his career Pistrucci was acclaimed and reviled in equal measure, maintaining a series of tense relationships with his colleagues, the most pointed of which with his fellow engraver William Wyon.

If we are to believe Pistrucci's version of events, it was his idea to have St George and the dragon as the design on sovereigns. His interest in the subject was aroused by Lady Spencer to whom he was introduced by Sir Joseph Banks. On behalf of her husband, she asked that Pistrucci make a model of St George in wax, her preference being for the composition to be in the Greek style, as opposed to a medieval treatment in which the saint could have been presented armed to the teeth and clad in metal. On completing the commission Pistrucci is reported to have then suggested the same design be adopted for the new gold coins of 1817. The difficulty with the story is that much of it comes from Pistrucci himself and there is good evidence to suggest he was not always a reliable witness to the events of his own life.

Saints in combat with writhing beasts had been part of the design of English coins since the introduction of the angel in the fifteenth century. St George had become the patron saint of England a century earlier, making his first appearance on the coinage on George nobles of Henry VIII in 1526 and he was also to be found at the centre of the Garter belt of Thomas Simon's Petition crown in 1663. Pistrucci's knowledge of such rare English coins was unlikely to have been all that formidable and the same might be said of his awareness of the few early eighteenth-century Italian coins which carried the same design elements but he might have been expected to know that St George was suspended from the garter belt on half-crowns of 1816. That George III was portrayed in a cartoon published in 1805 as St George protecting Britannia's honour from Napoleon in the guise of a dragon is some evidence of the popularity of the myth and there are medieval paintings of the subject matter to be seen on the walls of churches in Suffolk and elsewhere. St George was taken to symbolise the country by Shakespeare in *Henry V* and the revival of interest in the playwright led by David Garrick in the second half of the eighteenth century could have contributed to a popularising effect. It is evident, therefore, through one source or another that St George would not necessarily have been an obscure suggestion. Whoever actually generated the idea of having the saint on the gold coinage, and from what source of inspiration, may never be known for sure but in its realisation Pistrucci played a central role.

Above. Equestrian figures from the Elgin Marbles, showing the cavalcade on the west side, bear a strong similarity to Pistrucci's treatment of St George.

Left. Study for St George and the dragon in wax by Pistrucci, wax modelling being a common means by which designers of coins and medals would visualise compositions prior to engraving in steel.

Facing page. St George slaying the dragon was a popular subject for medieval church wall paintings, as demonstrated by this fifteenth-century fresco from St Gregory's Church, Pottergate, Norwich.

We do not have every letter that passed between Pole and his protégé on how the design developed but such a record does survive in relation to how the crown piece of 1818 progressed, carrying an adaptation of the same composition. What emerges is the presence of Pole at every turn. He bombarded the young artist with suggestions and instructions on how the design should be changed from the shape of the sword to the perceived ferocity of the dragon. His drive and intense involvement can have been no less for the new sovereign as it took shape and when it came to finishing the coin their relationship was written into its very substance through the insertion of their initials hidden within the detail of the design.

The official description, as reproduced in the Royal Proclamation of 1 July 1817, provides a general view.

> Every such piece of gold money to have for the obverse impression the head of his majesty with the inscription GEORGIUS III. D. G. BRITANNIAR. REX. F. D. and the date of the year; and for the reverse the image of St. George armed, sitting on horseback, encountering the dragon with a spear, the said device being placed within the ennobled garter, bearing the motto HONI SOIT QUI MAL Y PENSE, with a newly invented graining on the edge of the piece. The said pieces of gold to be current and lawful money of the kingdom of Great Britain and Ireland, and to be called a sovereign or twenty-shillings piece, and to pass and be received as of the value of twenty shillings of lawful money of Great Britain and Ireland, in all payments whatsoever.

Apart from the presence of Britannia, the preceding 100 years of coinage design had been almost exclusively heraldic. Set against the uniformity of the eighteenth century, sovereigns with their St George must

have seemed a startling addition and, indeed, such an approach would have been consistent with what Pole judged necessary to ensure the guinea and sovereign were in appearance as different as possible. The most likely source of inspiration for how the myth was brought to life is the Elgin Marbles. They had been put on public display by Lord Elgin in 1807 and Pistrucci, steeped as he was in the classical tradition and living in central London, must have beaten a path to their door. The horseman is naked and the art critic John Ruskin later considered it odd that the saint should be unattired going into such a violent encounter. George III's portrait also played its part in the creation of a classic, his hair curling wildly through an imperial wreath and the line of his neck elegantly couped. It is the image of a man in middle age, whose gaze is intense and whose features are drawn opulently but in reality George III was elderly, bearded and bald. Coinage portraiture has often been a vehicle for the idealisation of monarchs, or a very public means through which their vanity can be expressed. Although Pistrucci must have had an eye to his patrons, and Pole's involvement was ever present, here he was realising his own artistic ambitions. A neoclassical revival was in full swing in late Georgian London and the refashioned sovereign captured the mood impeccably.

A much more traditional fate awaited the first half-sovereigns issued in more than 200 years. All the powers of exuberance had plainly been expended on designing the larger coin and what emerged into circulation in September 1817 was an angular shield of the Royal Arms of a style not seen before or since. The Master, though, was as deeply involved as ever, being at one point quite upset space could not be found for his initials on the surface of the shield. Ensuring there was a fractional element to the gold coinage demonstrated forward thinking but, like its higher value partner, it found the first few years of life beset with troubles.

Above. Half-sovereigns of 1817 carried a traditional heraldic design on the reverse.

Below. The portrait of George III at the end of his life by Samuel William Reynolds contrasts sharply with the idealised view of the king by Pistrucci.

The Ricardo ingot plan

For all the virtues of its design, the task ahead for the new coin was daunting. Production of sovereigns, using steam-powered presses, had started towards the end of May 1817 but there were several connected problems that stood in the way of the new system and its effective operation, including the role of banknotes, the level of prices and not least the ongoing regard attaching to the guinea.

Through 150 years of use, guineas had become deeply rooted in the affections of the nation. Professional fees were expressed in them and an echo of their former glory is still dimly to be seen in the names of certain prominent horse races. The conscious decision to allow guineas to remain in circulation might have had something to do with a wish not to heap added pressure on those already feeling the squeeze from the new system. That sovereigns were lighter than guineas by one twenty-first part meant in effect there was no difference in the standard to which the two coins were struck and there was no great unease, at least on this point, about them circulating side by side. Guineas were still being passed in exchange during the following two decades but in time they started to enter the realm of fiction and equestrian prize money.

In the context of poor harvests, falling wages and the myriad of adjustments that were required after war, for many the return to gold had seemed like a heavy price to pay. Loss suffered in exchanging notes for sovereigns was certainly seen as a problem and once the new coins were available the response from the public was not, consequently, overly enthusiastic. A former Governor of the Bank of England, Jeremiah Harman, commented in February 1819 that 'people seemed indifferent about gold; that instead of coming to the bank for gold, they brought their gold to the bank'. On a number of occasions through the 1820s and 1830s challenges were raised on the basis that adopting gold had been paid for through hardship in the agricultural sector and some from the banking community, like Alexander Baring, continued to argue for the reintroduction of a bimetallic system.

Then there was the problem of the imbalance in demand for gold across Europe which had resulted in large quantities of sovereigns being exported to the Continent in the first few years of production. In 1819 the future Prime Minister Robert Peel indicated that, of the gold coined in France since October 1818, 75%, or £5 million, was believed to have come from British gold made during the preceding couple of years. So serious was the problem that the five-shilling silver crown, issued again in meaningful numbers from 1818, was enlisted to help supplement the needs of circulation. Although there was a moderate gap in value between sovereigns and crowns, it was not the first time such an expedient had been tried, the most recent instance being the release of countermarked Spanish dollars in 1797 and the nineteenth century was to see yet more as attitudes towards a circulating coinage of gold shifted.

In relation to banknotes, a great deal of political energy had been expended on agreeing when the war-time restrictions on converting notes into coins should be lifted and matters were not finally resolved until the early 1820s. With more sovereigns being produced the prominent role of lower value banknotes gradually started to wane and a defining moment came in 1826 with an Act of Parliament which prohibited notes in England and Wales below the value of five pounds. But the transition took time and banknotes formed a good proportion of the total cash in circulation for some years to come. As with all such boundaries between notes and coins, a clear commitment had to be made one way or the other to allow either the coin or the note to thrive. In Scotland low-value notes continued to be

Above. The political economist David Ricardo by William Holl, based on Thomas Phillips' engraving, 1839.

released by private banks and even into the mid-nineteenth century there remained a strong preference for notes over gold sovereigns north of the border. One commentator suggested that a genuine Scotsman should always prefer a dirty note to a clean sovereign.

Beyond questions of personal preference for guineas or paper, a more fundamental threat to the system came with the ideas of the economist David Ricardo, who was a firm and influential advocate of abandoning a circulating gold coinage altogether. Ricardo's proposition, as captured in a series of essays and pamphlets, was directed at encouraging the use of banknotes, with the proviso that when access to gold might be required it would be made available in much larger quantities than could ever be satisfied through coinage. His thinking was so compelling it found its way into draft legislation and during the course of 1819 into law with provision for 60-ounce ingots of gold being supplied through the Bank of England. On the basis of the prevailing price an ingot would have cost in the region of £233 – a considerable amount at the time. Apart from exceptional circumstances, the intention was for the nation's reserves to remain secure in the vaults of the banking sector, people relying on banknotes and silver for everyday exchange, with the objective of creating a more stable currency. As Ricardo put it, 'the use of precious metals as money was a great step in civilisation, but it would be another improvement to banish them again in our times of greater enlightenment'. Even while it was still trying to find its feet, therefore, the restored sovereign, for a short time at least, came close to being abolished.

A curious solution was trialled in the form of a round ingot about three inches in diameter, close to an inch thick, and consequently looking a little like a snuff box, with no fewer than four coinage portraits of George III on one side, four armorial bearings on the other and engraved around the edge the inscription BANK OF ENGLAND 60 OUNCES. The round version of the Ricardo ingot never entered production in anger, probably on account of its complexity arising from the presence of four separate coinage dies on each side contained within a metal housing, but a prosaic rectangular version did. By the end of February 1820 enough gold had been made available to produce 2028 ingots, which amounted to in excess of £470,000. In the event, however, only 13 were ever sold, a revealing indication of an absence of interest amongst the moneyed class. Whatever the government's

Above. Over 2000 Ricardo ingots, with their own individual serial numbers, were produced in 1820 in a rectangular form.

Below. In executing Ricardo's plan, the initial intention was to make the 60-ounce gold ingots available in a highly elaborate struck version.

thinking on the matter, lack of genuine support from the Bank of England ultimately deprived the experiment of the powerful financial ally it required and the Bank's own activities in buying gold to be turned into sovereigns eroded the basis of its operation. Although short-lived, the Ricardo ingot plan left in its wake a number of obscure artefacts, whose connection with the coinage seems at first tenuous, and also a great rarity in sovereigns of 1819, whose mintage of just 3574 was driven by holding off production in light of the plan's implementation. With ongoing legislation, the need to re-establish gold-using habits and arriving at an understanding of how many sovereigns should be produced, it was not until the tenth anniversary of Waterloo that the currency settlement of 1816 could be regarded as having properly established itself.

The loss of St George

Having secured the issue of silver and gold coins in 1817 it was necessary to resolve the design of double-sovereigns and five-sovereign pieces, what might be seen as the more ceremonial end of the coinage. Revisions made to the figure of St George for the crown piece of 1818 meant the patron saint now carried a sword in his right hand rather than a broken lance and, more importantly, every element of the composition had been considered afresh. Overall the impact was a low-relief sculpture of much greater refinement. *The Gentleman's Magazine* read into the design a good deal more than was probably intended, seeing an obvious allegorical reference to the 'genius and valour of Britain triumphing over the Demon of anarchy and Despotism', transmitting to posterity, 'a record of the great and brilliant events which, under Providence, have led to the restoration of peace and happiness throughout the world'. Changes to the appearance of St George found their way almost immediately onto the higher value gold coins but the design was amended further by removing the encircling garter belt. It was in this simplified form that St George and the dragon was to appear first on double-sovereigns and five-sovereign pieces under the name of George III, and then on sovereigns of George IV (1820-30). Four years had elapsed since an Italian gem engraver had been invited to design Britain's coinage and those few years shook up the traditions of a nation.

For George IV's first coinage Pistrucci created another neoclassical portrait, heroic in bearing and in its full features implying something of the appetites of the monarch. But even before Pole had left his position as Master in October 1823, the victim of a Cabinet reshuffle, his relationship with Pistrucci had begun to deteriorate, in part over the artist's unwillingness to copy a bust of the king by the sculptor Sir Francis Chantrey for a medal to commemorate a royal visit to Ireland in 1821. The incoming Master in 1823, Thomas Wallace, did not care for the existing range of designs across silver and gold coins and within the next few years several of those introduced at the time of the recoinage were swept away. Pistrucci's laureate portrait of George IV was ultimately replaced by Wyon's version of the Chantrey sculpture and the Italian's fall from grace accelerated when sovereigns were issued in 1825 bearing the shield of the Royal Arms. Silver crowns, too, which during the early 1820s had carried his St George now displayed a highly elaborate heraldic design. In the context of a wider renewal of the coinage, the removal of Pistrucci's designs was less personally directed than the coincidence of events might at first appear but that cannot have masked the sense he must have felt of tides turning against him. Although fêted in years to come, his St George was not sufficiently well liked at the time for it to be saved and heraldry was to dominate the face of sovereigns for the next half century.

Above. Laureate portrait by Benedetto Pistrucci for the first coinage of George IV (left), alongside the bareheaded portrait by William Wyon used on sovereigns from 1825 (enlarged).

Chief coin of the world

Design and circulation

After an uncertain start, output levels in the first ten years of issuing sovereigns and half-sovereigns reached close to £40 million, an indication of how the arrangements were becoming properly established. The design of sovereigns had been changed in the mid-1820s and the replacement of Pistrucci's portrait of George IV with a bareheaded effigy was to provide a template for future kings of Britain into the twentieth century, represented as they were, for the domestic coinage at least, without crown, gown or sceptre.

For several years Pistrucci had poured his creativity into the British coinage but William Wyon had been building his reputation and in 1828 it was he who secured the sought-after position of Chief Engraver. A decade later he was elected to the Royal Academy, one of very few engravers to be accorded such an honour, due recognition, it might be thought, of his ability to engrave the human form in metal which was abundantly clear from his Cheselden medal of 1829 and later the medals for the Great Exhibition of 1851. For the coinage one of his finest designs was his Una and Lion five-sovereign pattern piece, inspired by Edmund Spenser's sixteenth-century poem *The Faerie Queene*. Medallic in style, it depicts Queen Victoria (1837-1901) as Una guiding the British lion and has all the hallmarks of subtlety and poise to be seen in much of his other work. For the coinage in general circulation, his portrait of Victoria used from the early years of her reign on gold, silver and copper was also impressive. He was granted a sitting at Windsor towards the end of August 1837 and as a result prepared a wax model. His portrait transformed a monarch, not known for her beauty, into an attractive young woman. It is hardly surprising he became a favourite and that his Young Head portrait was retained until Victoria was in her late 60s.

Loss of the German territories of her Hanoverian forebears, on account of the exclusion of female succession in Salic Law, resulted in a change to the Royal Arms which from 1837 into the current reign have remained fundamentally the same. The shield sovereigns issued during her reign from 1838, depicting the Royal Arms surrounded by a wreath and an outer band of lettering, were handsome and fondly regarded. But although essentially a static type for over 30 years there were, almost inevitably, variations on a theme. There were the unexplained narrow-shield sovereigns in 1838 and 1843, which being struck in relatively limited numbers have become extremely desirable. Experimentation between 1863 and 1874 with die numbers, introduced to track the quality of poor output back to the press operator, meant the insertion below the shield of tiny numerals, acquiring a complete record of which has since become a ceaseless challenge for certain sovereign collectors. Related to but distinct from the die-numbered sovereigns are the pieces of 1863 bearing the numerals 827 in relief on the truncation of Wyon's Young Head portrait. So far only a few have come to light and it is now believed their existence relates to experiments into brittle gold obtained through Rothschild. The coins entered circulation, as did other sovereigns from a like experiment conducted at Tower Hill by George Ansell, the resulting pieces, dated 1859, being distinguishable by the presence of a small line in Victoria's hairband on the obverse. As with any extensive coinage, produced over several decades, the quality of striking ebbed and flowed. There were instances of dies continuing in production beyond their useful lifespan, resulting in

Above. The accomplished design of the Una and Lion five-sovereign piece of Victoria, 1839, has almost certainly enhanced its appeal above and beyond its rarity.

Facing page. An exquisitely modelled portrait of Victoria in wax by William Wyon, probably dating from the late 1830s.

coins bearing cracks or other defects. But the Victorian sovereign was manufactured, by and large, to stringent standards of weight and fineness, and given the numbers involved the level of consistency was remarkable.

Between 1817 and 1850 in the region of £94 million in sovereigns and half-sovereigns were struck. Coin manufacture can rightly be regarded as one of the first examples of mass production but the nineteenth century witnessed output on a truly industrial scale. Just as important, a strong indication that what was being produced was actually being used can be seen through information collected by the banking sector on the wear gold coins were suffering in circulation. As the banker and writer on coinage matters John Biddulph Martin explained, 'the life of a sovereign, like that of a man, is threatened by perils from two sources, violence or accident on the one hand, natural decay on the other'. It was the latter of the two that posed the greater problem for sovereigns. Value and metal content were still inextricably linked and allowing a situation to develop in which light sovereigns and half-sovereigns might build up would undermine confidence in the status of the currency, the very considerations that drove government to act on worn gold in the 1770s. As far as the post-1817 gold coinage was concerned, initially it was enacted that a sovereign would no longer be regarded as legal tender if its weight fell below 7.954 grammes, a full-weight sovereign being 7.988 grammes. For half-sovereigns the limit was set at 3.969 grammes, as against the standard weight of 3.994 grammes. The reality on the ground demonstrated such tight margins to be unworkable and in 1821 the lowest weights at which sovereigns and their halves could remain current were made slightly more generous. But with the loss still falling randomly on the last holder, human nature provided a powerful incentive for mass non-participation in observing the law and the problem of worn coins in circulation grew steadily more severe.

By the 1840s, upwards of 20% of gold coins tendered to the Bank of England were judged to be below the legal limit. Renewed efforts on the part of the authorities to maintain the condition of gold, and provide the means through which diminished pieces could be removed, took the traditional form of a standalone recoinage which started in 1842 and by 1845 had resulted in the exchange of roughly £14 million in sovereigns and half-sovereigns. It amounted to about a third of the estimated total population of gold coins and went a long way to improving the situation. Small numbers of guineas were also swept up in the initiative, surrendered from private hoards or, in some instances, probably still furtively passing from hand to hand. The presence of 18 guineas dating from between 1731 and 1794 in the Market Harborough hoard of 183 gold coins deposited about 1829, and discovered in 1971, points to their continued use alongside sovereigns. But while the active circulation of guineas ultimately came to an end the name never vanished. When Thomas Hardy, writing 40 years later, had his character Michael Henchard auction his wife in *The Mayor of Casterbridge*, the sum agreed with the sailor was five guineas. Names given to coins could, nevertheless, be interchangeable and there is some evidence from other literary sources to suggest the familiarity of using the term guinea might have led to its being applied to sovereigns.

Gold coins being tendered at the Bank of England in a worn state is compelling evidence that their practical function as a medium of exchange was being performed. Their appearance in hoards deposited during the nineteenth century provides additional confirmation and also points to other functions the coins were fulfilling. Several hoards containing gold coins were buried after 1817, such as the 731 found in April 1962 in Ramsgate, Kent, consisting of 615 sovereigns and 116 half-sovereigns struck between 1817 and 1850, the accumulation possibly having been laid down in the year of the last dated coin. Not only do hoards of this type reveal how long the coins were remaining in circulation, upwards of 30 or 40 years being common, but they also show the degree of wear suffered and raise thought-provoking, but sometimes unfathomable, questions about why the coins were deposited in the first place. As well as an anxious hiding of wealth at a time of crisis, it was often a way in which income was saved. Writing in 1861, but setting her story in the early years of the nineteenth century, George Eliot created in *Silas Marner* a character who existed at the extreme end of the hoarding spectrum: 'He had taken up some bricks in his floor underneath his loom, and here he had made a hole in which he set the iron pot that contained his guineas and silver coins, covering the bricks with sand whenever he replaced them. Not that the idea of being robbed presented itself often or strongly to his mind: hoarding was common in country districts in those days'. The psychology behind such a desire to hide away a lifetime's wealth will, likely as not, have still found a resonance 50 or 100 years later and what survives now of this record is, in a sense, the remnant of failed hoards not recovered by the owners compared with the many others that will have been laid down.

Domestic circulation of gold in Britain aided economic growth but as coinage gold had always been no respecter of borders and in the first half of the nineteenth century Britain consciously promoted use of sovereigns overseas, a currency extension of its imperial ambitions. Beyond the deliberate actions of politicians in London, however, the world took to using sovereigns because the coin was liked and trusted. It was the British sovereign that played a key role in the establishment of what came to be the most quintessential of American organisations, the Smithsonian Institution, forming part of the original endowment in 1838 of over 100,000 newly minted gold coins. The United States authorities are thought to have requested recently struck rather than previously circulated sovereigns because the bequest would thereby realise slightly more when the coins came to be melted down.

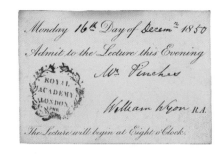

Above. A ticket from William Wyon inviting his former colleague John Pinches, who ran a prominent medal-making business, to a lecture at the Royal Academy.

Below. Portrait of William Wyon in plaster, 1851, by the German artist Wilhelm Kullrich who worked with Wyon for a time in London.

The currency of gold

For Britain the second half of the nineteenth century was a time of unparalleled prosperity, defined by a period of growth during which the country became the world's leading industrial and financial centre. From having been devastated during the Napoleonic Wars, the circulation of gold coins had recovered such that by the 1840s estimates suggest they outstripped banknotes in general currency. Following the additional restrictions arising from the Bank Charter Act of 1844, combined with increased output of gold, the difference between the two grew ever greater over the coming decades. Cash remained the preferred means of paying wages and ample supplies furnished retail trade but for larger transactions bills of exchange and cheques had long been employed. During the second half of the nineteenth century the banking sector assumed a more important role in personal and commercial affairs and the deposits built up came to be translated into cheques to a much greater extent. The gold standard played a part in anchoring the confidence and security of the broader system of payments, strengthened by industrial and trading performance but also contributing to it.

Almost certainly encouraged by the British model, by the 1870s several other western economies had adopted their own gold standards, including France, Germany, Switzerland, Belgium, Holland and, importantly, the United States. Sterling, though, was the epitome of a gold-standard currency and sovereigns were its embodiment. In 1887 it was reported to a Royal Commission set up to look into the depression of the 1870s that 'Britain is the only country in the world where there is a real gold standard, the only place where, if a man has a bill for £100, he knows what he has got, and he knows that in all cases he can obtain for his bill for £100 a certain quantity of gold at a certain weight and fineness'. How the design of sovereigns responded to sterling's higher profile was a mixture of the good, the bad and the ugly, well-intentioned mistakes sitting side by side with outstanding works of art.

As far as 'the good' was concerned, Britain's currency had been blessed with two remarkably talented engravers and what could be considered their finest work came when Pistrucci's St George was restored to the gold coinage in 1871, finding itself combined with Wyon's Young Head portrait of Victoria. Charles Fremantle was the Deputy Master behind the change which reflected his view that, 'it is hardly possible to over-rate the advantages accruing to a coinage from an artistic and well-executed design'. It was an inspired decision and, like Pole before him, Fremantle lived by an ambition to improve the appearance of all Britain's coins. For Fremantle his route to that end was by reissuing former designs, while for Pole it was to be found in commissioning new works of art.

What might be regarded as 'the bad' aspect of the nineteenth-century sovereign is reflected in the extent to which abuses of the coinage presented an obstacle to their circulation. Counterfeits were certainly known. Some of the best examples were those in gilded platinum emanating from Spain in the 1870s and the gilding of sixpences to pass as half-sovereigns in 1887, just as shillings had been likewise altered 300 years earlier under Edward VI, caused some anxiety. But in general such activities, while ever present, were never a major concern. In *Oliver Twist* (1837) Charles Dickens has Mrs Bumble's husband scrupulously examine a group of sovereigns 'to see that they were genuine' and similarly Fledgeby in *Our Mutual Friend* (1864) when counting out a number of gold coins 'rang every sovereign', which was a well-known means of assessing whether a coin was genuine and could, in part at least, help explain why sovereigns were not extensively counterfeited.

Above. Sovereign of Victoria of 1871 bearing designs by the great rivals Benedetto Pistrucci and William Wyon.

Below. Jubilee Head portrait of Victoria by Joseph Edgar Boehm on an 1887 double-sovereign.

Facing page. The reverse of Victorian shield sovereigns, the one shown is of 1853, was profoundly traditional but nonetheless beautifully composed and well executed (enlarged).

74

Admired though it undoubtedly was, Wyon's portrait of Victoria had been a feature of the coinage for almost 50 years and its longevity prompted some to reflect on the need for a change. But its eventual replacement with an effigy by Joseph Edgar Boehm, first issued in 1887, the year of Victoria's Golden Jubilee, was not at all well received. It became known as the Jubilee Head and, while describing it as 'ugly' might be a little harsh, it was from the start heavily criticised. The presence of a small crown, which Victoria was actually fond of wearing, has often been cited as the chief flaw in the composition but it was not the only weak link. Boehm, an accomplished sculptor, may have created a faithful likeness but the elements of crown, widow's veil and extended truncation drew attention to Victoria's pointed profile. No sooner had it been introduced on gold and silver coins than demands for its withdrawal were being made and it lasted only six years before the introduction of Thomas Brock's more sympathetic endeavours.

A feature of the Jubilee coinage in relation to sovereigns was their distinctive yellow colour. It was the result of deliberately adding more silver with the intention of making the coins slightly softer and therefore easier to strike to help cope with a larger scale portrait. The change in alloy came and went but of more lasting impact was the alteration to the die axis of the coins from being inverted to one in which the obverse and reverse were upright when rotated around a vertical axis, a modification which has been maintained through the following 130 years.

St George did not immediately vanquish the shield of the Royal Arms. Both types continued to be struck for a few years before production of sovereigns, in London at least, entirely dropped the heraldic approach from 1875. The Royal Mint's branches in Sydney and Melbourne, reference to which follows, continued to employ both designs until 1887 and in that same year use of St George was extended to five-sovereign and double-sovereign pieces. It was not until further changes to the coinage, introduced in 1893, that a half-sovereign was to carry the design and with it the suite of Britain's gold coins achieved the uniformity they were to retain for the next 100 years. *The Illustrated London News* described the new half-sovereign as 'vastly pretty' and *The Art Journal* referred to the design as having 'triumphantly borne the test of time'. With all that had happened to Britain's currency over the course of the nineteenth century, and its role in the vanguard of establishing gold as the standard to which all major economies aspired, the St George design had become a symbol of stability and, in some respects, of sterling itself.

The range of gold coins extended from half-sovereign to five-sovereign piece but in reality, as had been the case in the eighteenth century with the five-guineas and two-guineas, neither of the two coins valued above a sovereign ever played anything approaching a meaningful part in everyday life, an indication of which can be seen in the production of double-sovereigns in 1887 being the first mintage for over 50 years. At the other end of the range serious thought was given to a quarter-sovereign in 1853 as a way of providing an alternative to high-value silver coins. The Royal Mint at the time could not process gold and silver simultaneously and the idea had been that in periods of gold production striking quarter-sovereigns could act as a substitute for silver. Its impracticably small size, however, stood against its introduction and so the rather attractive pattern pieces produced to demonstrate what it could have looked like came to nothing.

Of the two main gold coins, half-sovereigns played a less important role internationally, serving a more domestic function and consequently being struck in smaller numbers. Wear rates recorded during the nineteenth century for half-sovereigns were always higher since the coin had a greater surface area in relation to its weight and was probably more roughly treated. Not only, therefore, did it survive less well, it was more likely to be lost in handling and was more difficult and costly to produce. Problems of wear were more extensive in relation to half-sovereigns but sovereigns suffered as well and, as an isolated exercise, the recoinage of the

1840s could never have been expected to provide a permanent solution. Carrying gold coins in spring-loaded cases helped limit the degree of wear but they were not for everyone and it was estimated that for sovereigns and half-sovereigns to fall below their minimum legal weights would take no more than 15 years. By the late 1860s 30% of sovereigns were thought to be below the least current weight and for half-sovereigns more than double that level. A further 20 years on and the problem had grown much worse, leading one commentator to suggest Britain's gold coinage was masquerading like 'a discarded servant in the livery of an old master'.

When the journey a sovereign could have taken during its life is considered it is not hard to appreciate why it would have become so degraded. Having been carried by tourists to Scotland or North Wales it might be called upon by farmers in the buying and selling of livestock or at harvest time, then transportation across to the east-coast fishing industries could follow and on to the manufacturing districts where the shortage of cash was often felt more acutely. Behind such a circuit of usage stood the railways but more importantly the regional network of banks, constantly facilitating the business of making currency available to their clients and it was they who saw at first hand the wear to which the gold coinage was being subjected.

Maintaining standards

It is conceivable government could have allowed matters to go unchecked as it had in relation to silver in the eighteenth century but the role played by gold was now too important domestically and, in view of Britain's key position in the world economy, the situation could not be allowed to continue. The scale of production, too, reflected how important a question the circulation of gold had become. As in the sixteenth century, discoveries had a major impact on the amount of coinage produced and when new supplies were unearthed in California in the 1840s the influence was soon to be observed through substantial increases in sovereign output in the early 1850s. Just shy of £140 million in gold coins were issued in the 25 years up to 1875, with a further £100 million being added before the end of the century.

Right. Weighing machines at the Bank of England provided an automated means of establishing whether a gold coin had worn below the legal limit. Bank officials referred to this process of weighing coins as 'machining'.

In 1889 an Act of Parliament was passed which established the important point of principle that the loss of value from wear should fall on the state rather than the last user. Thereafter a programme was set in motion to remove all pre-Victorian gold coins, subsequent provisions a couple of years later demonetising them altogether. That sovereigns from the beginning of Victoria's reign remain legal tender into the twenty-first century is a consequence of the reforms enacted at this time. Then, in the early 1890s, another government measure established a system of continuous recoinage, operated through the Bank of England, for sovereigns and half-sovereigns. To make the system work the Bank weighed every gold coin which passed across its counters, a formidable task made possible through the use of automatic balances actually designed by a former Governor of the Bank, William Cotton, some years earlier. The Royal Mint had been employing the balances from the mid-nineteenth century to weigh struck coins prior to issue and there is no doubt they made a significant contribution to the maintenance of accurate standards. Operating at the other end of the cycle the Bank came to rely on the machines to test the weight of coins and, ultimately, to judge whether or not they were fit for continued circulation. By the close of the century the estimates of wear had plummeted, standing at 4% for sovereigns and 10% for its half, the preceding decade having seen upwards of £40 million exchanged.

Those handling gold on a regular basis would therefore have seen an appreciable uplift in quality but that was also a reflection of the continuous work undertaken for some time to improve every element of manufacture. Fremantle, who was Deputy Master during the period 1868-94, had been a staunch champion of enhancing the quality of the coinage and for him it was never merely a case of establishing a standard and sticking to it. Rather, there was a constant striving to refine gold more accurately, to see more tightly controlled tolerances governing weight and to ensure the most up-to-date machinery was in place actually to strike the coins. Margins had been set so finely in relation to weight, use of the automatic balances as the final check on struck coins could, on occasion, see as much as 60% of half-sovereign output rejected. There was a sense, indeed, for a time in which the application of extremely tight controls had gone too far but it was endeavours along these lines that helped imbue sovereigns with their reputation for reliability.

Fremantle was helped in his mission by the highly respected metallurgist William Chandler Roberts-Austen. The framework Roberts-Austen was working within had been established by the Coinage Act of 1870 which had introduced comprehensive changes to regulations governing the accuracy of sovereign production. An example of the stricter limits was to be seen in weight and fineness margins being applied to individual coins rather than as before to bulk samples. It was from this time that the Trial of the Pyx, the centuries-old system for certifying the weight and metal

Above and below. Guillotine used at the Bank of England to score, and thereby deface, gold coins to be taken out of circulation.

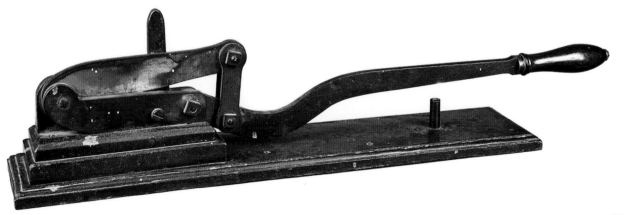

Above. Bronze plaque of Sir William Chandler Roberts-Austen by George William De Saulles.

composition of the nation's coinage, was held annually. The Royal Mint was thereby subjected to a greater degree of public accountability, a move further emphasised through the publication by the organisation of an annual report. Roberts-Austen rose to these challenges by making a series of improvements to the consistency and accuracy of how gold was melted and refined. One aspect of the advancements he made included introducing pure gold trial plates, against which the quality of coins was tested, having discovered that it was impossible to obtain a homogeneous mix of metals within such standard plates when using an alloy like 22-carat gold. Although the fine detail of experiments carried out in a metallurgist's laboratory might have seemed to most users of sovereigns profoundly esoteric matters, they nevertheless sat at the heart of the trust ultimately placed in the coin.

For all the care taken over producing sovereigns, what could not be denied was the extent to which the nation's wealth was literally being worn away between the fingers of its population and the consequent losses suffered to the Bank of England's gold reserves. David Ricardo's reasoning that a gold standard could be sustained without the need for precious metals to circulate ultimately underpinned a number of initiatives to limit the costs of the existing arrangements. As Chancellor of the Exchequer in 1886, Lord Randolph Churchill was an outspoken supporter of withdrawing the half-sovereign altogether to be replaced with higher value silver coins, and the release of double-florins in 1887, alongside crown pieces, was evidence of government seeking ways in which use of silver over gold could be encouraged. Serious consideration was also given in the early 1890s to the introduction of a one pound note. George Goschen was by then Chancellor and advanced the case for the banknote solution partly on the grounds that a circulating gold coinage was a luxury Britain could ill afford. He remarked that he 'would much prefer for national and monetary purposes to have £20,000,000 of gold under our command at the Bank of England than 30,000,000 sovereigns in the hands of the public'. Set against that was the extraordinary weight of tradition and the profound desire there was for gold as coinage, which had woven itself into the popular consciousness. Double-florins never caught on and Goschen's note proposal ultimately foundered on fears from within the banking community that the system would be undermined by large-scale forgery of banknotes. Sovereigns and half-sovereigns, therefore, emerged unscathed in the face of serious political and economic challenges, and in the 1890s Britain consciously chose to sustain an expensive system of coinage.

Sovereigns overseas

There were clearly self-interested motives underpinning the decision to maintain the status quo, not least the desire for continued stability and the Treasury itself saw a benefit to British commerce in the circulation of sterling at home and throughout the world, even if that meant supporting a policy which seemed at times overly charitable. The use of British gold overseas was extensive and had become more so as the century advanced. Countries bearing no allegiance to Britain, such as Brazil, Portugal and Egypt, came to regard sovereigns as their own currency, an expedient and compliment almost certainly born out of familiarity and confidence the coin commanded on account of the exacting standards to which it was made. When the *SS Central America* sank in September 1857, sailing between San Francisco and New York, it was carrying a large quantity of gold coins, the majority made in the United States, but a fair proportion were sovereigns, the earliest dating back to 1823, which will have been in circulation in some sense in California. A flavour of the coin's international profile from a literary source some 40 years later, drawn no doubt from real-life experience, is provided by that most travelled of writers, Joseph Conrad, who sprinkled through his novels set in South and Central America

references to sovereigns being stored by ships' captains as ready cash. Closer to home politically, a list drawn up in the second half of the nineteenth century named 36 colonies and dependencies in which British gold was legal tender. According to the artist Theodore Spicer-Simson, based on knowledge of his father's independent business interests and associations with the Rothschild bank, sacks of sovereigns were transported to some of the most inaccessible parts of India and, apparently, not one was ever lost.

Although on the surface of it the British currency was being accorded an honour through its extended use abroad, many sovereigns, like those forming the foundation bequest of the Smithsonian, will have promptly found themselves back in the melting pot and likely as not eventually being turned into sovereigns all over again. The Royal Mint and the Treasury were well aware of their Sisyphus-like labours but saw a wider interest in benefits ultimately accruing to the British economy.

Another dimension to the imperial nature of Britain's currency arose as a result of discoveries of gold in Australia in the mid-nineteenth century. A need to process the metal into a transportable and tradable form led to calls from Australia itself for the establishment of a mint close to where the gold was being found. In 1853 the lobbying paid off and two years later a mint was opened in Sydney, as an overseas branch of its parent in London, being granted the authority to strike sovereigns and half-sovereigns to the same standard of weight and fineness as those issued since 1817. The building chosen for the Sydney Mint was a former hospital erected in the second decade of the nineteenth century during Major-General Lachlan Macquarie's tenure as Governor of New South Wales. It became known as the Rum Hospital, having been built as part of a deal with a consortium of businessmen through which they funded construction in return for securing a contract to import 45,000 gallons of rum to sell to the colonists. Senior staff who ran the mint were selected in London, such as Charles Elouis, the Registrar and Accountant at Tower Hill, who became the Superintendent of the Bullion Office in Sydney and, with army officers already manning mints in India, the Deputy Master was to be Captain Edward Ward, of the Royal Engineers.

There were, initially, reservations about the proposition arising from concerns the coins would not be produced to a sufficiently high standard. To counteract the perceived reputational threat, output from Sydney was initially legal tender only in certain colonies and the design was deliberately different from Royal Mint sovereigns struck in London, bearing as it did AUSTRALIA set within a wreath, SYDNEY MINT above and ONE SOVEREIGN below. Production difficulties were certainly encountered, such as the inability to arrive at the correct balance within the approved alloy. The gold being mined had a high silver content, as much as 5% or 6%, which could not initially be refined out locally, resulting in sovereigns of a distinctive yellow colour. But the upside was these same coins were to prove extremely popular in India, partly because of the colour, there being a contrast with the slightly redder hue of those produced in London.

After a few years, however, any anxieties there were about quality of output had been laid to rest and from 1866, following a positive report from

Above. Sydney Mint sovereign of 1904 showing the S mintmark (enlarged).

Below. Unambiguous reference to the origins of the coin was a distinctive feature of the early Sydney Mint sovereigns.

Facing page above. The gold trial plate of 1829 was used for several decades in the nineteenth century for sovereigns produced in London and Australia.

Facing page below. Photograph album presented to William Hocking following his visit to the Perth branch mint in 1908.

Below. From 1871 sovereigns struck overseas were distinguishable by extremely small mintmarks on the ground line. From the top: sovereigns minted in London, 1871; Sydney 1904; Melbourne, 1904; Perth, 1904; Canada, 1911; India, 1918 and South Africa, 1928.

a Select Committee of the House of Commons, the coins were declared legal tender in Britain. The distinctive design continued for the time being, a further aspect of its difference being the portrait of Victoria by Leonard Wyon, William's son. Almost certainly intentional, the Queen's hair was wreathed in native banksia, a neat numismatic allusion since the flowering shrub had been named after naturalist Sir Joseph Banks who had been heavily involved in reform of the currency in the early nineteenth century and in ensuring gold sovereigns formed part of the settlement after Waterloo. As it became more firmly established Sydney was allowed from 1871 to strike sovereigns bearing the same design as those of London but carrying the distinguishing S mintmark. The Royal Mint, far from leaving the new operation to fend for itself, took its duties of supervision seriously, demonstrated by directly supplying from London the individual dies used to strike the coins and insisting that reports be submitted back on a regular basis. Quality standards were monitored through the furnishing of sample coins to London and Captain Ward even took out with him a portion of the 1829 gold trial plate so that he could more correctly ensure the gold in Australian sovereigns was of the correct standard.

There were soon calls for another mint to be established, satisfying very much the same need as had led to setting up the Sydney branch, and the location chosen was Melbourne. Rather than adapting an existing building, the Melbourne Mint was purpose built and, with official confidence in production standards having already been proven, it was permitted from the outset in 1872 to strike sovereigns of the same design as those minted in London, but again distinguished by the insertion of a mintmark, in this case M. Establishing a pattern of links between branch mints that was to be repeated on several occasions, Captain Ward was transferred from Sydney to run the Melbourne Mint, a clear endorsement of his abilities and recognition of the need for experience. As with Sydney it was equipped from Britain and the same levels of supervision were applied with all dies being prepared and shipped from London. Once properly up and running Melbourne was to make a significant contribution to the total number of sovereigns produced and thereafter in active use. Indeed, with its sister operation in Sydney, before the end of the century the output of the two Australian mints amounted to about 40% of the gold circulation in the Britain. It represented more or less the same proportion in which the coins were actually made and demonstrated the indiscriminate nature of their passage through the late nineteenth-century world.

A mint in Perth was opened in 1899 to service the huge discoveries of gold in Western Australia, its sovereigns bearing a P mintmark, and in 1908 a further branch started production in Ottawa in Canada as a result of gold finds in the Yukon, the letter C distinguishing its coins. From the outset the Ottawa Mint, as well as making sovereigns for circulation internationally, had responsibility to strike coins for domestic use but demand was never as strong as elsewhere and its 628,000 pieces made only a small contribution to the overall scale of output. The same point can also be made in relation to the mint established in Bombay in 1918 but, nevertheless, in the single year of its operation more than twice the number of sovereigns were made, bearing the I mintmark, than in over a decade at Ottawa. Finally, in 1923, a branch mint was opened in Pretoria and its large output of sovereigns all carried the SA mintmark. Connections between Australian branch mints continued with further exchanges of staff, allowing knowledge to be shared and contributing to a consistency of output across what was now a global network. Regular contact was sustained with London through correspondence as well as occasional visits such as that by William Hocking, Assistant Superintendent of the Operative Department, to all three Australian branch mints in 1908 to audit and recommend improvements to their accounting procedures. He recorded the lengthy sea voyage to

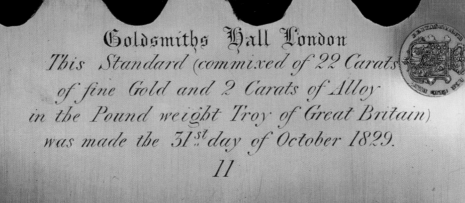

Goldsmiths Hall London
This Standard (commixed of 22 Carats
of fine Gold and 2 Carats of Alloy
in the Pound weight Troy of Great Britain)
was made the 31st day of October 1829.

11

Australia, together with his observations once there, in a personal journal and as a memento of his visit the staff at Perth prepared an album of photographs which stands as a valuable visual record of the mint during the first decade of the twentieth century.

The cultural life of sovereigns

It is known that sovereigns were used extensively as currency in the nineteenth century because of the sheer numbers struck, their presence in the hoard record and the large quantities of worn specimens needing to be withdrawn from circulation. As in Tudor times, though, they had a counterlife as objects of desire or as gifts, as a means through which a favour was rewarded or as the manifestation of a lifetime's wealth.

The coin's role in many aspects of nineteenth-century life was in part related to higher wages and increases in prices. From being the preserve of monarchs, gentlemen and the monied class in Tudor England, sovereigns had come firmly within the reaches of the middle class. For many in late nineteenth-century Britain, however, 20 shillings was a large amount of money and for the poorest third of the population, who at the best of times struggled to survive, a sovereign will have been a rare sight. In circumstances where a pint of beer cost about threepence and a pound weight of cheese about tenpence it is clear that a sovereign could still purchase a substantial amount of food and drink, suggesting its use was less likely centred on small individual purchases than it was on settling bills for bulk transactions or items of a more expensive nature. For those who found regular work the level of pay, even lower down the income scale, could provide for a sustainable if not an abundant life. A building labourer in the south of England might have expected to earn just over £40 a year and a stonemason in the same part of the country about £65, which would have meant a sovereign was in the region of a week's income for members of the labouring class. Installing gold coin changers, machines designed to give change for sovereigns and half-sovereigns in silver coins, probably in the lobbies of hotels or London clubs, suggests that handing over to a cab driver or shopkeeper a single coin worth several days' pay would not have been appreciated. That a sovereign would have generated a good deal of change is colourfully expressed by Mr Mantalini in *Nicholas Nickleby* (1838) when he dramatically exclaims, 'I will fill my pockets with change for a sovereign in halfpence and drown myself in the Thames'.

The sheer number of sovereigns being transported around the country to pay wages in government dockyards or in manufacturing towns, transacted through the hands of cattle dealers or grain merchants, conveyed by tourists to the seaside resorts of Sussex or Devon and ultimately being reconciled by the national network of banks and post offices is strongly suggestive of extensive usage by a sizeable proportion of the population. For those higher up the income ladder, such as a junior clerk in the banking sector with an income of at least £150 a year or a principal clerk on between £700 and £900, the coin will certainly have been familiar. Senior civil servants, such as the Secretary to the Post Office, would have received a salary in the region of £1700, placing them firmly in the bracket of those for whom higher value gold coins had become eminently affordable.

What functions sovereigns performed, other than being spent directly, can be discerned from anecdotes and in the pages of the nineteenth-century novel. It is said, for example, that the Duke of Wellington always carried with him a number of sovereigns which he would give to veterans of the Battle of Waterloo should he ever meet them whether on the streets of London or elsewhere in the country. The survival at Stratfield Saye of a black leather wallet belonging to the Duke, replete with sovereigns of the 1840s,

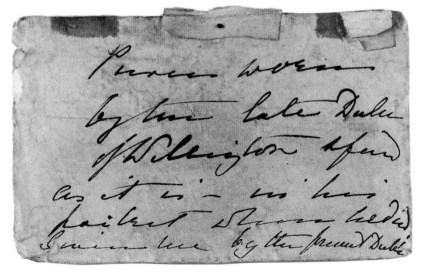

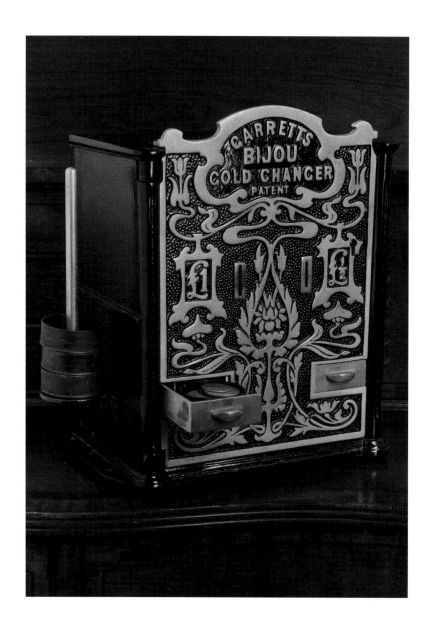

lends weight to the story which is itself consistent with other known instances of his generosity to those with whom he served.

Gold coins found their way into the fictional narratives being written about a rapidly changing Britain and, in contrast to the sixteenth century, sovereigns were integrated into these stories in a way that suggests the coin was very much part of many people's lives, both in exchange and in a more emotional setting. Writing in 1860 George Eliot in *The Mill on the Floss* provides an insight into a tradition of giving sovereigns as a present. Tom Tulliver says to his sister Maggie, 'I don't want *your* money, you silly thing. I've got a great deal more money than you, because I'm a boy. I always have half-sovereigns and sovereigns for my Christmas boxes because I shall be a man, and you only have five-shilling pieces, because you're only a girl.' The Tullivers, at least before their financial problems, would have been regarded as well off and there are many other references to sovereigns throughout the story in relation to savings or as a coin someone might readily have about their person. A sense of everyday familiarity, however, was often tinged with a certain level of emotion. What is conveyed is the impression of an object readily met with yet prized as with Amelia in William Thackeray's *Vanity Fair* (1849) when she presents to her mother 'her silver, and her sovereigns – her precious golden sovereigns'. A parable of how a sovereign was valued over and above its monetary worth is relayed by E. M. Forster in *A Room with a View*, published in 1908. Having temporarily borrowed some change to pay a cab fair from Freddy Honeychurch and his friend, Miss Bartlett is eager to settle her debts to them straightaway when the two boys suggest tossing a coin for who would have her sovereign. 'Please—please,' she protests, 'I know I am a sad spoilsport, but it would make me wretched. I should practically be robbing the one who lost.'

As part of what people would save, sovereigns were hoarded for a rainy day and thus it was that Tess, in *Tess of the d'Urbervilles* by Thomas Hardy, published in 1891 but set during the depression of the 1870s, finds herself falling back on her stock of sovereigns and, when they were all gone, found herself unprovided for. The great social chronicler Charles Dickens is often more keen on employing guineas but in making reference to sovereigns, and more so half-sovereigns, he illustrates how they inhabit the lives of his characters. When Monks is paying Mrs Bumble for information in *Oliver Twist* (1837) it is in sovereigns that the deal is conducted, 25 of them. But the coin could equally be encountered as a symbol of trust, its reputation for quality filtering into the literary imagination as when Joseph Conrad in *Lord Jim* (1900) has Charles Marlow describe Jim as looking 'as genuine as a new sovereign'.

The spectacle of a group of gold coins could have a magnetic impact above and beyond their pure monetary worth. Writing to his parents having found out he had sold *Treasure Island* to the publishers Cassell for £100, Robert Louis Stevenson could barely contain his excitement on receiving the fee in sovereigns: 'a hundred jingling, tingling, golden, minted quid'. Liddy in Hardy's *Far from the Madding Crowd* (1874) is mesmerised by such an accumulation as was Mr Wilfer in Dickens' *Our Mutual Friend*, and for Tom Tulliver's father in *The Mill on the Floss*, after he had fallen on hard times, simply looking at a little store of sovereigns in a tin box 'seemed to be the only sight that brought a faint beam of pleasure' into his eyes. For those like bankers who handled sovereigns in a routine way the relationship would have been more functional. Again from *Vanity Fair*, at the premises of Hulker, Bullock & Co, bankers of Lombard Street, the cashier Mr Quill engaged in the benevolent occupation of handing out crisp banknotes from a drawer but dispensing sovereigns out of a copper shovel.

Literature of the time conveys the practical purpose of economic exchange but offers the added dimension of what sovereigns actually meant to people, as a means through which trust or suspicion could be expressed or as a way of painting a picture of debt-encumbered longing for a better life; wealth, poverty or status was defined and the presence of sovereigns reveals a cultural impact of far greater value than money.

From its uncertain reintroduction in 1817 the gold sovereign had come a long way, carving out a role for itself in almost every part of the globe. By the end of the nineteenth century Britain's circulating gold coinage, although costly, was a thing of beauty to behold. But within little more than a decade there was yet again the impending threat of war and with it the familiar uncertainties for a precious metal coinage engendered by major economic disruption and huge financial commitments.

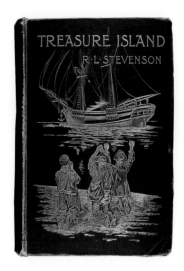

Above. Robert Louis Stevenson received 100 sovereigns from Cassell for *Treasure Island*. The designer of this front cover of the book, Walter Paget, was the father of Humphrey Paget who designed several United Kingdom coins and medals in the mid-twentieth century.

Impact of war

Removal from circulation

In the years leading up to 1914 the circulation of sovereigns in Britain was more extensive than at any time before or since and the huge numbers struck made the gold standard a reality for all but the poorest. The dominant position Britain had enjoyed in the second half of the nineteenth century in trade and finance continued on into the Edwardian era, bolstered by a sympathetic network of low tariffs between trading partners. Reflecting the economic reality, production of sovereigns continued apace during the first 15 years of the twentieth century, with annual output of gold regularly above £10 million and from 1910 more often than not exceeding £20 million. The highest yearly output, prior to the First World War, was seen in 1912 when just under £33.5 million in gold was processed, more in a single year than in the whole of the seventeenth century. On the eve of the outbreak of war the combined production of sovereigns and half-sovereigns in London and overseas since 1817 had reached the figure of £900 million and it was estimated that the circulation of gold in Britain in 1914 was close to £100 million.

In retaining the figure of St George engaged in his eternal battle with the dragon, the design of sovereigns under Edward VII (1901-10) and George V (1910-36) remained largely unchanged from the last years of Victoria. Differences in the portraits, however, between the two kings exerted an influence not just on the appearance but also on the actual production of the coins. The Royal Mint's engraver George William De Saulles had built for himself a reputation as a respected numismatic designer of the late Victorian period, so that with the accession of Edward VII there was an experienced artist on hand to prepare a new royal portrait. He did not disappoint. Edward's robust profile, occupying the greater part of the surface area of the coin, is every bit that of the distinguished-looking monarch.

George V's reign in 1910 brought with it the requirement for a new effigy and from the start the king had fairly strong views about who the artist should be. Bertram Mackennal was an Australian sculptor of considerable distinction, already having secured commissions in Australia and England, including the Boer War Memorial in Islington of 1903. George V was a confirmed fan and encouraged Mackennal's involvement when the coinage portrait was being commissioned. What emerged was a likeness of some sensitivity, an additional endorsement being its adoption on postage stamps and paper money. On the other hand, from a technical point of view it presented some problems brought about by Mackennal's having modelled the portrait at too high a relief. The resulting imbalance between the two sides of the coin created a ghosting effect whereby an outline of the effigy on the obverse appeared on the reverse. Subsequent efforts to alleviate the problem never quite worked and it stood as a salient lesson to those involved of the virtue in securing from the outset of any new coinage a technically sound effigy.

The proportion of the money supply made up by coins had declined from about a quarter in the mid-nineteenth century to just over 10% on the eve of war, the shift acting as an acknowledgement of the growth in importance of paper instruments of currency backed by the banking sector. But there was for those who continued to handle gold on a daily basis, as

Above. Edward VII by Baron Adolph de Meyer, 1904.

Facing page. Obverse of Edward VII sovereign, 1902, engraved by George William De Saulles (enlarged).

there had been for centuries, a visceral attachment. In the words of Lord Randolph Churchill, the handling of a gold currency instilled something 'very unfathomable and mysterious' and a century of resolving and managing all the problems generated by maintaining gold coins in circulation, capable of being used by large numbers of people, represented an achievement of which the nation could rightly be proud. Freshly minted, good-weight sovereigns were encountered on a regular basis and there is no question that their presence in people's lives was a source of pleasure extending beyond the economic into something much more personal.

There had been a downward trend in prices during the 1880s and 1890s, and although they had started to pick up again in the years leading up to the First World War they had not quite returned to the levels of the 1870s. What a sovereign might, therefore, have been able to buy had probably not advanced a great deal over that period and it would, in the natural order of such matters, depend on social rank. At the Cheshire Cheese pub on Fleet Street in London a sovereign would have fed eight people on steak and kidney pie, washed down with a pint of beer each, but for two to eat in more lavish style at the Café Royal would have required the possession of at least four sovereigns and a couple of half-crowns.

When they were not being spent on the necessities or luxuries of life, they were on occasion still being buried in large quantities in the ground for later retrieval. A relatively large number of coin hoards was deposited in the later nineteenth and early twentieth centuries, one example being that of 200 sovereigns and 16 half-sovereigns found in Twinstead, Essex, secreted in about 1912 and recovered in 2011. Between 1912 and 1915 there are at least 12 hoards of gold coins, one of the largest being from Wantage in Berkshire found in 1968 consisting of 264 coins deposited around 1915. War will have motivated some of these deposits, but there are sufficient numbers of others several years earlier to require alternative explanations of a less geopolitical nature.

Below. A large queue of people formed at the Bank of England on the eve of the First World War in the summer of 1914 to change their banknotes into gold coins.

The outbreak of hostilities in the summer of 1914 changed the British currency forever. Tensions between European powers had been growing in the month following the assassination of Archduke Franz Ferdinand on 28 June 1914 and as the air of crisis built towards the end of July banks sought to hoard their gold. Rather than paying those withdrawing cash in sovereigns, which was the usual practice, they paid them in Bank of England notes and, at five pounds, the lowest value note was far from the most practical of denominations for everyday transactions. A sense of anxiety over the solvency of banks grew and on Thursday 30 July, ahead of the summer bank holiday, large queues formed outside the Bank of England demanding to have their five-pound notes converted into sovereigns. Following newspaper reports of what seemed like a run on the nation's central bank, pressure was brought to bear on the rest of the banking sector. From having gold reserves of £27 million on Wednesday 29 July, the Bank of England found itself with less than £11 million by Saturday 1 August. The bank holiday was extended for a further three days to help the government deal with the crisis and meetings in the Treasury day and night resulted in a number of measures being agreed, one of the more innovative of which was the issue of Treasury notes for ten shillings and one pound to ease demand for half-sovereigns and sovereigns. They became known as Bradburys, the name deriving from the presence on the notes of the signature of John Bradbury, Permanent Secretary to the Treasury. Britain declared war on Germany on 4 August and when the banks reopened on 7 August the expected demand for cash deposits in gold did not materialise, people heeding the exhortations of government ministers to stop using gold and readily accepting the new Treasury notes.

There was, though, no formal suspension of gold in 1914 as there had been in February 1797 arising from the threat of a French invasion but the government urged people instead in the strongest terms to stop using sovereigns. If there had been a tendency to regard a precious metal coinage

Below. The so-called 'Bradbury' one pound Treasury notes came to be readily accepted as part of emergency financial measures connected with the outbreak of the First World War.

THE BRITISH SOVEREIGN WILL WIN

INVEST IN THE WAR LOAN TO-DAY

ASK FOR DETAILS AT NEAREST POST OFFICE

as pandering to a collective national emotion, such an indulgence could not be sustained at a time of war. Lloyd George, the Chancellor of the Exchequer in August 1914, stated very forcefully right at the start of the conflict that those who sought to withdraw gold from banks were as good as helping the enemy by limiting the financial means by which Britain could fight. As such, gold disappeared quite simply because it became unpatriotic to demand it in payment.

By the summer of 1915 sovereigns had largely disappeared from the streets of London, the result of speeches by government ministers and a more general sense of people supporting the war effort in whatever way they could. Government propaganda was not just directed at encouraging the population to enlist but also to invest in national loans and the posters often drew upon coinage imagery to press home the message. Emotively, silver coins were depicted as turning into bullets and if there were any doubt about how strongly sovereigns had come to be associated with the person of the monarch, the link was forcibly made through the medium of government-backed propaganda. The sovereign had been invented 400 years earlier as a personal statement of kingship and now on the eve of its removal from circulation the personal connection was refashioned for a new audience, served up as art for posters to help fight a war. Sovereigns continued to be struck for another two years, with 1.5 million being produced in 1916 and a million the following year, but these mintages were historically small.

The position, however, was not the same in every part of the world, especially for those who had come to rely heavily on sovereigns. There was, for example, a need to establish a branch mint in Bombay in 1918 to produce sovereigns directly connected with the exigencies of the time. One of the more conspicuous areas in which their continued circulation actually helped the war effort was the Middle East. British Army officer T. E. Lawrence, popularly known as Lawrence of Arabia, was given by government many thousands of sovereigns as a means of buying the loyalty of those he encountered. It was a wise move. Every tribesman, it was said, would have sovereigns knotted into their clothes and the coastal towns in particular were awash with British gold. Deeper meanings were there to be elicited too, Lawrence himself providing a colourful example when he described inviting a sheikh, as a gesture of gratitude, to thrust his hand into a bag of sovereigns, allowing him to keep all he could hold. The sheikh regarded it as the last word in splendour but Lawrence knew it to be a fairly economical gesture since it never cost him more than £120.

In the years immediately following the outbreak of war an important moment was reached in the history of precious metal currencies. Active circulation of gold had coincided with Britain's pre-eminent position economically, militarily and politically, and in regular usage being brought to an end lay a severing of the link with centuries of tradition. What had started under Edward III more than 500 years before was now over and Britain would never again see gold coins used as the medium of exchange in the everyday setting of markets and pubs. John Bull's feeling 'twice the man' when he jingled gold in his pocket had been written out of history by the most devastating of conflicts. Britain's position as the dominant world power was also at an end as America grew ever more influential. The war crippled the country financially and that decline was reflected symbolically and actually in the loss of its intrinsic-value currency. It was retained for a time with silver but even there the standard was reduced to almost half its previous sterling level within 18 months of the Armistice. Money's modern age had dawned and with it base metal and paper reigned within the circulating medium.

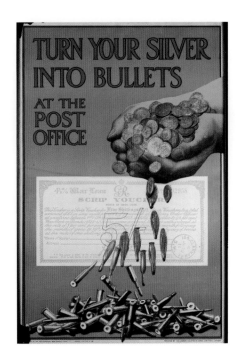

Above. Eye-catching poster encouraging the public to contribute to Britain's war effort.

Facing page. Government loan posters of the First World War made emotive reference to gold sovereigns.

The gold standard revisited

But as with all good stories, there was a sequel. Despite its absence from an active circulating life in Britain, the history of the gold sovereign was far from over. Production at Ottawa went on until 1919 and the Australian branch mints continued striking into the 1920s, with minting at Sydney coming to an end in 1926, Perth and Melbourne stopping in 1931 and the final branch mint, established at Pretoria in 1923, continuing to make sovereigns until 1932. During the early 1920s, with the exception of Perth, output was limited and the circumstances in which the Melbourne and Sydney coins were made had more to do with backing paper money than for actual circulation. Such pieces would therefore have been locked away in vaults and it was only in South Africa where, although sovereigns were produced principally for export, they at least circulated locally because mine owners insisted on paying their workers in gold.

In Britain, too, the coin's role in the currency system had a reprieve. Since the pre-war system had offered unprecedented stability and prosperity there had been a general expectation the country would return to gold after the war. The Cunliffe Committee on Currency, which reported in 1919, had been in favour and it was thought less a question of whether sterling should return to gold than when. Winston Churchill, as Chancellor of the Exchequer, had agonised about the policy, consulting widely, but in his Budget statement of April 1925 he finally resolved to recommend bringing Britain back onto gold but with sovereigns as a reserve rather than a circulating currency. He quickly regretted the decision, regarding it as the biggest mistake of his life. As after Waterloo, the plans had been formulated following a devastating war, and in suggesting bullion should be made available in relatively large amounts, in the form of bars, it looked very much like David Ricardo's ideas had been resurrected. The Royal Mint's Deputy Master in the 1920s, Robert Johnson, summarised the new arrangements in typically forceful fashion when he noted how they would not involve a circulating gold coinage because that would have been 'an unwarrantable extravagance in which our present financial position would not allow us to indulge'. Instead the Bank of England would be obliged, if called upon, to redeem its notes in bars of bullion containing 400 ounces of fine gold, the value of a bar at the time being about £1700. A small quantity of sovereigns was struck dated 1925 in connection with re-minting light gold for the Bank of England but production soon stopped and the coins never saw the light of day in exchange.

Other countries followed Britain back onto gold, including France, Italy, Norway and Portugal but, even as a diluted gold standard, in Britain the policy was perceived as having a hugely negative impact on the economy. The second half of the 1920s was characterised by deflationary forces and prolonged levels of high unemployment. When Wall Street collapsed in October 1929 it caused a major crisis in world trade and by September 1931, faced with an inability to shore up the value of sterling, the British government's adherence to gold had to be abandoned in the wake of mounting recessionary forces and a heavily debt burdened Exchequer. Britain was not alone. Other countries that had adopted the gold standard in the second half of the nineteenth century had to abandon the position in the early 1930s. Devaluation for the pound became inevitable and in looking for someone to blame Churchill came in for particular criticism but, as is so often the case in politics and economics, it was more a matter of timing than of a profoundly unsound idea. The Royal Mint melted down 90 million sovereigns during 1930 and 1931 to turn into bars of standard gold for the Bank of England. It would be difficult to find a more potent and poignant symbol of the end of an era than to see the coin's original manufacturer being ordered to destroy the product of its own labour.

Those sovereigns to escape the melting pot, and they were moderately large in number, went on to play a role in the international movement of gold between markets, particularly between London and other key financial centres. They were hoarded, too, because people knew they could rely on the weight and fineness of a sovereign and in uncertain times their importance in that regard was always enhanced. In addition, the ceremonial function of the coin remained intact. Years after his previous unfortunate brush with sovereigns as Chancellor, when Churchill as the great war leader presented the Sword of Stalingrad to Stalin in 1943, he accompanied it with a sovereign, the tradition being that the gift of a cutting edge must include a token payment to avoid cutting the friendship between the two. The coin, then, never lost one of the first functions it performed, that of its role in ritual over and above its use as money.

Below. The *News Chronicle* of 21 September 1931 led with the story of Britain's abandonment of the gold standard.

News Chronicle

POSTAGE : in U.K., 1d. ; Canada, 1d. ; Abroad, 1½d.

No. 26,654   LONDON   MONDAY, SEPTEMBER 21, 1931   MANCHESTER   ONE PENNY

BRITAIN OFF THE GOLD STANDARD

"The ultimate resources of this country are enormous and there is no doubt that the present exchange difficulties will prove only temporary"—Cabinet Statement

BILL THROUGH BOTH HOUSES OF PARLIAMENT TO-DAY

£200,000,000 WITHDRAWN FROM LONDON IN THE LAST TWO MONTHS

STOCK EXCHANGE CLOSED

BUT BANKS OPEN AS USUAL

Mr. Ramsay MacDonald hurrying into No. 10, Downing-street on his arrival from Chequers yesterday.

BANK RATE
6%

SURPRISE SUNDAY DECISION TO RAISE IT

HIGHEST SINCE 1929

AN increase of the Bank rate to six per cent. was announced last night by the Bank of England.

A meeting of the Cabinet was held at No. 10, Downing Street, last evening, and the following communique was issued immediately afterwards:

His Majesty's Government have decided after consultation with the Bank of England that it has become necessary to suspend for the time being the operation of Subsection '(2)' of Section 1 of the Gold Standard Act of 1925, which requires the Bank to sell gold at a fixed price.

'A Bill for this purpose will be introduced immediately, and it is the intention of His Majesty's Government to ask Parliament to pass it through all its stages on Monday, September 21.

In the meantime the Bank of England have been authorised to proceed accordingly in anticipation of the action of Parliament.

The reasons which have led to this decision are as follows : Since the middle of July funds amounting to more than £200 millions have been withdrawn from the London market.

is passing the necessary legislation. This will not, however, interfere with the business of the current settlement on the Stock Exchanges, which will be carried through as usual.

His Majesty's Government have no reason to believe that the present difficulties are due to any substantial extent to the export of capital by British nationals. Undoubtedly the bulk of the withdrawals have been for foreign account.

They desire, however, to repeat emphatically the warning given by the Chancellor of the Exchequer that any British citizen who increases the strain on the exchanges by purchasing foreign securities himself or assisting others to do so is deliberately adding to the country's difficulties.

Mr. Snowden, Chancellor of the Exchequer, will broadcast at 9.15 this evening from all stations of the B.B.C. a talk upon the situation revealed by the official communique.

Sir Oswald Mosley Stoned

From Our Own Correspondent
GLASGOW, Sunday.
Sir Oswald Mosley, leader of the New Party, was mobbed by a hostile section of a crowd of 15,000 which gathered on Glasgow Green this afternoon, and after his speech he had some difficulty in making his way to his car.
Sir Oswald was struck on the head by a stone, but was not seriously injured.
Three members of the platform party

WHAT IT MEANS

BANKS' STRENGTH UNIMPAIRED

BUSINESS AS USUAL AT HOME

By a City Correspondent

IN plain words, the temporary abandonment of the gold standard by this country means that we are ceasing, for an indeterminate time, to settle our international payments in gold.

In the world of commerce different forms of currency are adopted in each country, such as pounds, dollars, francs, etc., which may be regarded as a means of purchasing national goods, but when it comes

LATE NEWS

An alternative life

Yet other strands to the ongoing existence of the coin remained, some of them as adventurous as the design on the coin itself. During the Second World War the contents of the survival kits of Special Operations Executive agents included sovereigns, the thinking being that such operatives would have the means to buy or bribe their way out of tricky situations should the need arise. There is something of a parallel with the use to which T. E. Lawrence was putting the coin 25 years earlier and its real-life role militarily, and for the security services, was to find expression in related works of fiction.

When Ian Fleming was looking to give James Bond something with which he might extricate himself from danger he turned to the familiar gold coin. In his 1957 novel, *From Russia with Love*, Bond is given a briefcase by Q Branch containing 50 rounds of 0.25 ammunition, a flat throwing knife, a cyanide death-pill (which Bond washed down the lavatory), the silencer for a Beretta and hidden in the lining, 'in case hard cash was needed, the lid of the attaché case contained fifty golden sovereigns'. In the film version of the novel, travelling on the *Orient Express* Bond is confronted at gunpoint by the villain, Red Grant, and, as a way of distracting his assailant, Bond offers to pay for a cigarette with the 50 sovereigns. He withdraws them from the briefcase, housed in two leather straps and through one or two additional twists and turns the lure of the famous gold coin is ultimately Grant's undoing. For Fleming the association of Bond with the right brands, be they clothes, cars or hotels, was part of his agent's identity and the choice of the gold sovereign will have reinforced the same message. The actual briefcase from the film, remarkably, survives but alas not the two leather straps or, as far as is known, the 50 sovereigns.

James Bond's possession of the coin had a parallel in reality in the Royal Air Force of the 1990s. During the first Gulf War when British fighter pilots were sent on missions over Iraq, as well as all manner of relevant kit it might be imagined a modern fighter pilot would need to survive, their equipment included sovereigns taped to their chests so that airmen if shot down behind enemy lines would have the wherewithal to bargain their release.

Below. Scene from the 1963 James Bond film *From Russia with Love* in which Q issues Bond with a briefcase containing 50 gold sovereigns hidden inside the lining.

When it could have been thought that with its removal from circulation, and the prevailing conditions of economic disruption following the Second World War, the gold sovereign would never again play a meaningful role in the life of the nation, the tide turned in its favour. In a sense the disruption of the post-war economy drove interest in gold precisely because it had acted as a refuge in troubled times. There was a level at which such an instinct drove personal behaviour but there was also a global dimension. The Bretton Woods system of fixed exchange rates, which had been established in the summer of 1944, tied the value of the dollar to gold and, since all major currencies were linked within the system, gold through the dollar played an important role in acting as a force for stability in the post-war world. Still being employed in international markets, therefore, sovereigns started to command a premium above their gold value on account of their scarcity, which in turn attracted counterfeiters to take advantage of the favourable margins. Their activities, on a reasonably large scale especially in Italy and Syria, continued for many years and such was the quality of their work, both in relation to gold content and appearance, the coins became difficult to detect. Around the illegal production there naturally grew up a support and distribution network, and within a short period a counterfeiting industry had developed, fed by demand for gold sovereigns emanating from the Middle East and the Far East but with major European centres also playing a role.

In reaction to the changed circumstances, in 1957 the British government launch a two-pronged attack, on the one hand by seeking prosecutions in the courts through the energies of the Treasury Solicitor and on the other by authorising production of the coin to supply the bullion market which was justified, according to a familiar press release of the time, on the grounds of meeting a manifest demand, 'which if unsatisfied might give rise to counterfeiting'. It had always been a coin with an international profile but this now became its chief function rather than an adjunct to a more central domestic purpose. As a way of maintaining manufacturing skills, but more so to meet known requirements, there had been strikings of the coin in 1949, 1951 and 1952 all bearing the date 1925. Applying a fixed date to new production had been a feature of other international bullion coins, such as the Maria Theresa Thaler, which has kept the date 1780, but such a practice was undertaken in relation to sovereigns with some misgivings. The more continuous mintages from 1957 involved new dates for each year of issue and between 1957 and 2014 approaching 90.6 million sovereigns have been made.

Above. Detail of the reverse of the 1957 sovereign (enlarged).

Below. Two counterfeit sovereigns purporting to be of Victoria and George V.

Beyond the requirements of the bullion market there continued the
tradition of preparing special sets of coins on the accession of a new
monarch. In the post-First World War era, the first to whom the practice
would apply was Edward VIII and had he remained on the throne beyond
December 1936 that tradition would certainly have been upheld. His
decision, though, to step down as king meant a great deal of the work
involved in preparing designs for his prospective coinage had to be shelved.
There is very little about his short time on the throne that is not wrapped
in one controversy or another and the coinage was no exception. His
portrait was the work of Humphrey Paget, an accomplished sculptor in his
own right who had been engaged in numismatic commissions since the
1920s. It was a technically sound portrait and a flatteringly attractive
likeness, its only problem being that from the point of view of British
coinage tradition Edward was looking in the wrong direction. Since the
reign of Charles II monarchs have been depicted on the coinage facing the
opposite way to their immediate predecessor, a convention Edward would
have ended because he viewed his left profile as his better side. The handful
of five-sovereign pieces, double-sovereigns and sovereigns produced as
pattern coins bear the Paget portrait and the St George reverse and,
although conspicuous by their fabled rarity, in every other respect they form
an element of the well-established design template.

As part of a wish to move swiftly on from the palpable mood of trauma
pervading the nation in the aftermath of the abdication, Paget was
commissioned to prepare the official coinage portrait of the new king,
George VI (1936-52). It proved every bit as well executed as that for Edward
and, with little else needing to change in relation to the gold coinage,
arrangements were put in place fairly smartly. Sovereigns struck in 1937,
the Coronation year of George VI, nonetheless, have the distinction of a
plain edge instead of the more usual milling, to emphasise their special

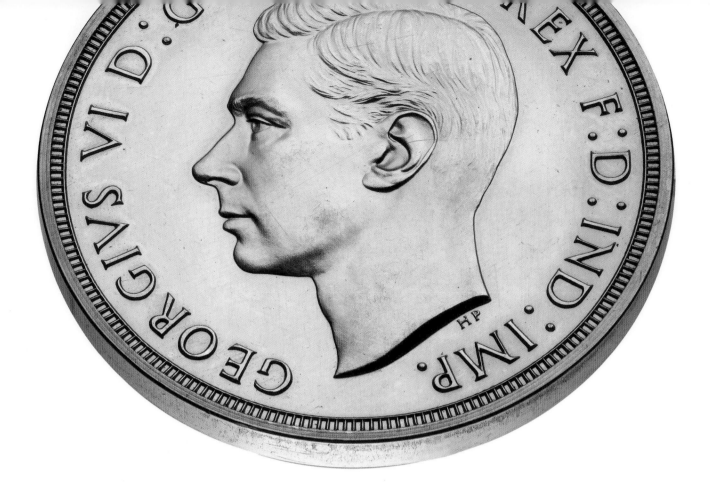

character as coins intended explicitly for collectors rather than for circulation. In light of the nature of the edge, the coins should strictly speaking be referred to as pattern pieces since the authorising Royal Proclamation only detailed types bearing a milled edge.

The advent of collecting as a more popular pursuit since the eighteenth century has stimulated an interest in Britain's principal gold coin and the importance that has attached to the rarity of sovereigns since the First World War is a central part of the coin's ongoing story. Unlike sovereigns of his elder brother, those of George VI were produced in sufficiently large numbers for them to be regarded as collector coins, a term that cannot be applied in any meaningful way to the first gold coins of Elizabeth II. A set comprising a five-sovereign piece to a half-sovereign was produced in 1953 deliberately to sustain the tradition of striking gold coins at the start of a new reign. But only a very few sets were ever made for distribution to major public museums, as well as the Royal Collection, none being produced for more general consumption amongst the collecting fraternity.

While the reverses of silver and base-metal coins changed with the accession of each monarch, the gold coinage through the twentieth century remained of a fixed type. The portrait side was, though, a different matter, and it fell to Mary Gillick to prepare the effigy of the Queen, probably the only occasion in British coinage history when this most prominent of commissions has been executed by a woman. It was a sensitive portrait, almost certainly influenced by Renaissance medals, depicting the Queen wreathed and modelled with a subtlety of line not seen since Wyon's effigy of Victoria. While it was replaced as part of the transition to a decimal currency on sovereigns and circulating coins with an equally accomplished portrait by Arnold Machin, it has remained in use on Maundy Money possibly because it is so fondly regarded.

Above. Five-sovereign pieces of George VI, 1937, had the same distinctive plain edge as sovereigns (enlarged).

The decimal era

Decimalisation

The changes wrought to the coinage as a result of decimalisation were brought together in the Coinage Act of 1971. In it the striking of sovereigns, and other gold coins, is specified and provided for such that, being enshrined in primary legislation, stability and continuity could be ensured. Operating like an indenture of former times, the Act defines precisely the weight and fineness of a sovereign. In one respect its position as a pound coin was to be expected but it was now, for the first time, made up of 100 pence as against the 240 pennies of the duodecimal age, and its 20-shilling identity had thereby been discarded. The retention of the gold coinage, made up of the same coins produced in the last years of George III's reign, maintained a link with Britain's currency history at a time when the nation was acclimatising to the brave new decimal world. Specifically in relation to the gold sovereign, the provisions of the Act could be seen as recognition of the coin's successful reintroduction in 1957, confirmed through regular issues over the course of the following decade. It left, however, the somewhat anomalous position intact that sovereigns struck under Victoria, and every monarch since, are still legal tender.

Moving to a decimal system of currency impacted on the location of where the nation's coins were to be made. The confined nature of the Tower Hill site combined with the need to build up a huge stockpile of decimal coins led to the building of a new Royal Mint outside London and the location chosen was Llantrisant, South Wales, 15 miles outside Cardiff. From the late 1960s production was maintained between the two mints but that sovereigns were the last coins in regular production in London in 1975, and were therefore the final ones to be minted at the historic site, is fitting.

Bulk production of bullion-standard sovereigns from 1957 was at the direction of the Bank of England but from 1979 output came to be supplemented by higher quality pieces specifically struck in limited numbers for collectors and the following decade witnessed several changes which redefined the gold coinage. Since that time, and particularly from the late 1980s, the market for commemorative coins has grown substantially, and sovereigns have occupied a not inconsiderable element. Rather than solely being the preserve of celebrations marking the accession of a new monarch, sets of gold coins, struck to an enhanced standard, have been issued regularly which speaks of a healthy demand in Britain as well as in many other parts of the world. From the start of the 1980s the sets came to include five-sovereign pieces and double-sovereigns, the first time they had been minted since the 1950s. Half-sovereigns were added to the portfolio at the same time, bulk production of which had not been seen since the First World War. The Royal Mint, in addition, was allowed to sell bullion sovereigns and half-sovereigns direct to consumers rather than the trade having to be directed through the Bank of England.

During such a period of change there was, however, no talk of ousting St George from his familiar place on the reverse of the gold coinage but there was a new portrait, this time by the sculptor Raphael Maklouf. It was deliberately from a tradition of portraiture which honoured the projection of an ideal of monarchy, directed at capturing not necessarily the precise wrinkles and expression of an individual at a particular moment in time but rather at conveying a more ageless impression.

Above. Pencil sketch of the Queen by Robert Austin for the one pound notes of 1960.

Facing page. Sovereigns showing the five principal coinage portraits of Elizabeth II. The artists who created the effigies are, from the top, Mary Gillick, Arnold Machin, Raphael Maklouf, Ian Rank-Broadley and Jody Clark (enlarged).

Britannia and commemorative coins

Above. Reverse of a one ounce Britannia bullion coin designed by Philip Nathan, 1987.

Below. Gold Britannia coins designed by Royal Academicians Christopher Le Brun, 2007 (top) and David Mach, 2011.

Starting with the South African Krugerrand in the 1960s, to be followed by the Canadian Maple Leaf, the Australian Nugget and the American Eagle, a new breed of gold coin had begun to appear in the market. While familiarity with the weight of a gold sovereign had nurtured loyalty, at 7.988 grammes, from a certain perspective it was a less than convenient amount. What the new bullion coins had in common was a coincidence of weight and, at one ounce of fine gold, they were appealing to the convenience arising from the unit in which gold was quoted and traded across the globe. The introduction of Britannia bullion coins in 1987 was directed at capturing a part of that market and, as it were, modernising Britain's precious metal coinage in line with international trends. In this context, Philip Nathan's design for the reverse was pitched at exactly the right level; it established a connection with the past in referencing De Saulles' standing Britannia from florins of Edward VII but, through the etiolated treatment of the national symbol, provided a modern view of female beauty. Nathan created a range of additional designs from the late 1990s, all on the theme of Britannia, and since then other artists have been commissioned, amongst them some highly regarded figures, including the Royal Academicians Christopher Le Brun and David Mach.

From December 2012 Britannia coins were produced in fine gold, as against the previous 22-carat standard. The link severed at the time of the Civil War in the mid-seventeenth century with a fine gold coinage had thereby been re-established. At the same time, a decision was taken to freeze the design of bullion coins, drawing very much on the idea of the historic popularity of fixed types, and it was Nathan's elegant original that was chosen. Collector versions of the coins, with an annual change of design, also formed an element of the new approach, an eye firmly fixed on satisfying the continued interest in Britannia as a theme.

When the new generation of British bullion coins was first seen in 1987 the future of the historic sovereign might have been thought in serious doubt – there was certainly no guarantee sovereign production would continue. But what has been notable about the intervening years is that Britannia gold coins have come to be regarded as an addition to rather than a replacement for sovereigns. Decisions taken in the 1980s to reintroduce the existing range of sovereign-related denominations, prior to the first release of Britannia coins, meant when the one-ounce revolution hit there were already in place the foundations of a new beginning. The coin with a good deal more history on its side has remained anchored in the tastes and preferences of those who handle gold not just for its value but also for its beauty. Since the position of the gold sovereign started to shift in the late 1970s a sense of dignified renewal has been apparent which has enabled a tradition to be continued in the face of challenges.

Production of special crown pieces to mark important moments in national life started in earnest in 1935 on the occasion of the Silver Jubilee of George V. A handful of like coins populated the next 50 years, instances of which included the crown piece to commemorate the death of Winston Churchill in 1965 and the Queen's Silver Jubilee in 1977. But these have been supplemented by more frequent issues since the early 1990s. In addition to the crown piece, the 50 pence and later the two-pound coin have become vehicles for commemorative themes embracing royal, scientific, literary, social, military and sporting subjects. The sovereign remained exempt until 1989 when, confronted by the 500th anniversary of its own introduction by Henry VII, a change in design was effected for one year only. Created by the sculptor Bernard Sindall, it consciously married the boldness of the original double-rose reverse with an enthroned portrait of the Queen which he had originally devised for the Silver Jubilee crown of 1977. On that previous occasion his designs had not won through but now, combined with beautifully composed lettering – a well-proportioned modern version of the late fifteenth-century Lombardic script – he had found a composition that worked.

The length of the Queen's reign, as with Victoria and George III, has required questions to be asked about how the image of the monarch ought to be updated. In the late 1990s the matter was resolved in favour of the introduction of a new portrait by the eminent sculptor Ian Rank-Broadley. In contrast to the timeless approach adopted by Maklouf, Rank-Broadley

Below. Sovereign struck for its own 500th anniversary in 1989 designed by the sculptor Bernard Sindall (enlarged).

Above. Drawing by Timothy Noad, with model, for the Golden Jubilee sovereign of 2002.

Below. The Jubilee sovereigns issued in 2002 and 2012 drew on distinct traditions within the coin's history, representing modern interpretations of the shield of the Royal Arms and St George and the dragon.

created a royal portrait at a definite moment in time, capturing a lady in her 70s, elegantly attired and decorously expressed. For the artist it was the fulfilment of a long-held ambition and in the approach taken, through the large lettering and a scale of portrait deliberately intended to fill the field, it was a conscious acknowledgement of the tradition of numismatic art best articulated by Benedetto Pistrucci through his effigy of George III on sovereigns of 1817. Such points of reference are not idle speculation. As a student of British coinage history, Rank-Broadley was intent on providing for a new generation a flavour of a golden age of design.

Beyond the periodic changes of portrait, if a special sovereign were to be issued for any occasion the Golden Jubilee in 2002 would be counted as amongst the most appropriate and Timothy Noad's shield of the Royal Arms represented a dignified response, at the same time paying tribute to the familiar Victorian shield sovereign. Noad prepared an additional sovereign design in 2005 but the next most prominent moment was to be provided by the Diamond Jubilee in 2012. On that occasion the sculptor Paul Day created his own version of St George and the dragon, eschewing admirably any sense of living in the shadow of a well-known Italian predecessor.

While sovereigns were being produced to mark a small number of specific events, the need for renewal of a different order became more irresistible. Pistrucci's original design had been engraved direct into late Georgian coinage steel, probably by Pistrucci himself once he had mastered the skill to work in metal. In the wearing out of tools and the requirement to have them re-engraved, the design over the years had become gradually less subtle, less accomplished and less like the work of art it had formerly been. Almost 200 years after its first appearance, a line had come to define the shape of the horseman rather than a seamless form rising from the table of the coin and so, in an effort to return to what had been originally intended, in 2009 tools from the reign of George III were employed to create new dies, a key feature of the initiative being to retain the differences between the denominations present on the original coins. It is for this reason that Pistrucci's name is written out in full on the gold five-sovereign piece and just his initials BP on sovereigns but here, too, there are several nuances in how elements of the design are rendered. On half-sovereigns St George had appeared only from 1893 and so it was tools from that period which provided the starting point. Fundamentally the composition has not changed but, for those who study the detail closely, the result has been to improve immeasurably the quality and to effect a restoration to the coin's former glory. There has also been a change in relation to the terms used to describe multiples of a sovereign, five-sovereign piece being an adjustment consciously made in recent years to reflect the practice of a previous age. Richard Sainthill, a respected numismatist of the mid-nineteenth century, used the term in 1842 in a letter to *The Literary Gazette* when he referred to 'the five-sovereign of Queen Victoria, the noblest coin in the English series'.

The group of denominations with reference to sovereign in their titles had remained the same since the coinage reforms of George III but an addition was made in 2009 through the introduction of a quarter-sovereign. Attractive pattern pieces of such a coin had been produced in 1853 as an exploration of the boundary between low-value gold and higher value silver coins. That territory's margins have long been a battleground of the British currency, also apparent in the ongoing division between coins and banknotes. In this instance, the presence of quarter-sovereigns offered to collectors of gold coins a wider range and their issue was not hindered by the needs of handling in everyday transactions which had stood in the way of the coin's introduction 150 years earlier.

In more than one respect the history of gold coins in Britain over the last 650 years is a reflection of the organisation that has produced them but one feature more than most stands out. Neither manufacturer nor coin would have survived into the modern world had they not adapted to the circumstances in which they found themselves. For sovereigns that has meant reductions in weight, alterations in fineness and a myriad of design changes. The Royal Mint, similarly, has needed to embrace innovation at keys points in its history, whether through the new technology of horse-drawn rolling mills or steam-powered coining presses, or in that most traditional of skills, engraving the portrait of a reigning monarch. Digital design technology has advanced to the extent that when a new effigy of Elizabeth II was being sought in 2014 conventional plaster models were competing alongside artwork developed chiefly using a computer sculpting programme. Through an anonymous judging process, managed by the Royal Mint Advisory Committee under the chairmanship of Lord Waldegrave, a portrait by young engraver Jody Clark, realised digitally, rather than through the traditional media of clay or plaster, won and sovereigns were amongst the first coins to carry the new effigy released in March 2015.

Below. Relief model by the sculptor Paul Day depicting St George and the dragon for Diamond Jubilee sovereigns of 2012.

Flight to gold

When Henry VII created a coin of 20 shillings he was for the first time introducing a single piece of gold to represent the pound sterling – the unit of account. The nature of what that denomination has been in terms of size, weight, metal content and name has changed but from 1489 until the First World War there was always a coin in circulation in Britain more or less equating to a pound. Banknotes came to play that role as well, particularly in times of war, and did so as a regular feature of the British currency from 1928 in the form of Bank of England one pound notes. Inflation washes at the shores of any currency system, quite literally eroding the size of precious metal coinages and wearing away established boundaries between banknotes and coins. By the early 1980s it had become clear through its short life in the wallets and purses of the population that the one pound note was not the most economical form in which this value should be expressed and the obvious alternative was to introduce a coin that would, by comparison, have an expected lifespan of 40 years. The outcome was the nickel-brass one pound coin produced from 1983 and with it, once again, the circulating unit of account was to be represented by a coin.

Although notes denominated as one pound continued to circulate through the private issues of banks in Scotland and Northern Ireland, the one pound coin, very similar in diameter if not thickness to the modern sovereign, proved to be enormously popular. Its success, unfortunately, stimulated the interest of the counterfeiting community, a shadow which has stalked any successful coinage since the idea of metallic currency was invented 2600 years ago. In recognition of the problem, and as part of a process of continuous review and modernisation, in March 2014 the Chancellor of the Exchequer, George Osborne, announced that a new one pound coin would be introduced in 2017, shaped like a pre-decimal 12-sided threepence, and carrying within its substance a raft of the most up-to-date security features.

Precious metal coinages throughout the world have been heavily influenced by instability, be that military, political or economic, and as often as not all three forces working in concert. Reliability of standards has always helped to instil trust but in times of extreme uncertainty a coinage's viability can be called into question or the uses to which it is put can shift. An impending threat of conflict can often be the explanation behind why hoards of coins are tucked away or in economically troubled times precious metals can seem like the last refuge of financial security. The global financial crisis which erupted in 2008 saw a great many question the nature of their wealth and the form in which it was held; it can be no coincidence that demand for bullion sovereigns increased significantly in the years following and annual production has since been sustained at robust levels. Historically always an area where sovereigns have been popular, the Mediterranean basin proved again to be one of the chief sources of demand, with Greece in particular representing a sizeable element.

A further initiative, reflecting the enhanced global appetite for gold, has been the return to production of sovereigns overseas. From the time of the establishment of the Australian branch mints, India has been a ready market for the coin and the precedent of sovereigns having been struck in Bombay, even if only for one year during the First World War, was important in determining a location for overseas production. An awareness of how overwhelmed the Indian market had become with counterfeit sovereigns also stimulated a desire to redress the balance in favour of the genuine article and, as a way of supplying the demand direct, a relationship was established in 2012 with the Swiss company MMTC PAMP India which maintains a production facility in New Delhi. Since 2013 sovereigns have been produced annually and in 2014 half-sovereigns were added, the coins being ——ble, as previously, with the I mintmark.

Above. The last Bank of England one pound note issued prior to the release of the one pound coin featured Sir Isaac Newton.

Below. The initial floral series of one pound coins was designed by the eminent silversmith Leslie Durbin who years earlier had worked on the Sword of Stalingrad.

Facing page. A gold necklace of traditional Indian design incorporating several Victorian shield sovereigns.

Facing page. Reverse of a modern sovereign of Elizabeth II, 2015 (enlarged).

Indian attachment to sovereigns can be seen not just in the sense of formal currency but also in use of the coins in jewellery, whether as earrings, necklaces or a myriad of other forms of decoration. Throughout the world sovereigns, as with almost every other type of coin, have performed functions above and beyond the call of duty, coming to be employed as a means of weighing or a symbol of good luck, as a source of metal for a dentist or a talisman to ward off ill-health, as a means through which to disseminate a message or a way in which to choose who goes into bat in a cricket game, as the marker of a building's age in a time capsule or as the end piece for Black Rod's staff in the Palace of Westminster. While the function of the gold sovereign has shifted from circulation to collector, the production in limited numbers of the coins in modern times is not a great deal different from the deliberate striking of presentation pieces for Henry VII in the late fifteenth century. In both instances what is being satisfied is the desire to possess the means through which to give or admire a well-made object in gold.

Conclusion

For those who handled gold sovereigns to pay their rents, their workers or their restaurant bills there is sufficient testament to know the transactions had greater meaning than the sums involved. Gold possesses some remarkable qualities and for these seemingly to be invested in the form of a coin created a beguiling relationship, charging moments of exchange with significance. The economist John Maynard Keynes might have regarded gold in the form of currency as 'a barbarous relic' but there were others who saw in it 'the guarantee of good faith'. Making coins in gold to circulate as currency was lending to the essentially utilitarian the quality of a treasure and it was, perhaps, the discreet pleasure taken in that understanding which made the difference.

From its origins under Henry VII the gold sovereign has diminished in size and fineness but not in beauty. Indeed some would argue that the modern sovereign, still bearing its 200-year-old portrayal of St George slaying the dragon, is bathed in splendour not less than the original. Its very name from the outset has carried a personal connection with the monarchy and through over 20 royal accessions, as well as a seismic shift or two in the nation's currency arrangements, it has retained its status as the unit of account. Somewhat shorn of its political overtones and no longer shouldering the reputational weight of the gold standard, the coin today provides a living link with the past, projecting back over 500 years how it has witnessed, represented and, in a modest way, influenced events.

The high point of Britain's gold coinage is undeniably to be found in the eighteenth and nineteenth centuries, both guineas and sovereigns providing the monetary basis for an expanding British empire alongside a commercially dynamic economy. Yet challenges were almost always present. Maintaining a gold coinage in good condition carried a heavy cost and the idea, indeed the reality, of allowing a proportion of the nation's wealth to be worn away in the everyday action of business and exchange exercised minds on a regular basis. Threats of war arose to challenge its existence. Threats, too, from currency reform and changing customs, from the theories of economists and the prevailing economic climate raised questions about its survival. Somehow, though, it has survived and particularly for the gold sovereign the reality of being anchored almost as much in the heart as in the purse has defined its character and made it immeasurably more than money.

Output of sovereigns, 1817-1974

Output of sovereigns for each year, in £ millions, excludes five-sovereign pieces, double-sovereigns and half-sovereigns. The figures are taken up to 1974, the date of the last sovereign produced at Tower Hill and prior to the more regular issue of proof sovereigns.

A. Royal Mint

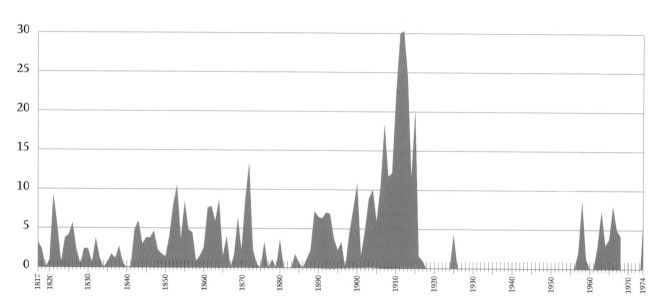

B. Branch mints

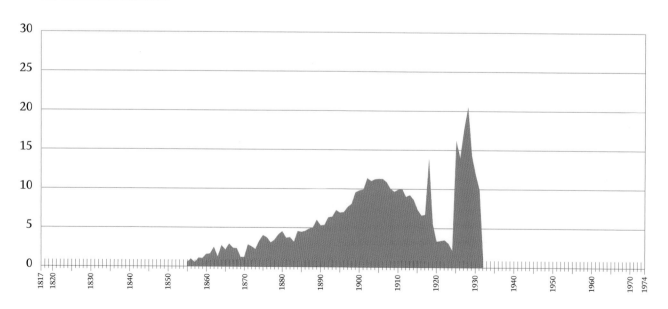

Designers of gold sovereigns

Monarch	First Issued	Obverse Type	Artist	Reverse Type	Artist
George III	1817	Laureate	Benedetto Pistrucci	St George	Benedetto Pistrucci
George IV	1820	Laureate	Benedetto Pistrucci	St George	Benedetto Pistrucci
	1825	Bare Head	William Wyon	Shield	Jean Baptiste Merlen
William IV	1830	Bare Head	William Wyon	Shield	Jean Baptiste Merlen
Victoria (London)	1838	Young Head	William Wyon	Shield	Jean Baptiste Merlen
	1871	Young Head	William Wyon	St George	Benedetto Pistrucci
	1887	Jubilee Head	Joseph Edgar Boehm	St George	Benedetto Pistrucci
	1893	Old Head	Thomas Brock	St George	Benedetto Pistrucci
Victoria (Sydney)	1855	First Head	James Wyon	Wreath	James Wyon
	1857	Second Head	Leonard Charles Wyon	Wreath	James Wyon
Edward VII	1902		George William De Saulles	St George	Benedetto Pistrucci
George V	1911		Bertram Mackennal	St George	Benedetto Pistrucci
Edward VIII	*unissued*		Humphrey Paget	St George	Benedetto Pistrucci
George VI	1937		Humphrey Paget	St George	Benedetto Pistrucci
Elizabeth II	1953	First portrait	Mary Gillick	St George	Benedetto Pistrucci
	1974	Second portrait	Arnold Machin	St George	Benedetto Pistrucci
	1985	Third portrait	Raphael Maklouf	St George	Benedetto Pistrucci
	1989	500th anniversary	Bernard Sindall	500th anniversary	Bernard Sindall
	1998	Fourth portrait	Ian Rank-Broadley	St George	Benedetto Pistrucci
	2002	Fourth portrait	Ian Rank-Broadley	Shield	Timothy Noad
	2005	Fourth portrait	Ian Rank-Broadley	St George	Timothy Noad
	2012	Fourth portrait	Ian Rank-Broadley	St George	Paul Day
	2015	Fifth portrait	Jody Clark	St George	Benedetto Pistrucci

Branch mints, except Sydney up to 1871, followed the London types from the start.

Bibliography

The intention throughout this book has been to offer a general view of the presence in circulation of the gold sovereign and how it has interacted with the world. It is hoped the following list of publications will give to those with a more sustained interest a means through which to explore the subject matter more thoroughly.

Richard Aldington, *Lawrence of Arabia. A Biographical Enquiry*. London, 1955.

Martin Allen and D'Maris Coffman (eds), *Money, Prices and Wages. Essays in Honour of Professor Nicholas Mayhew*. 2015.

G. F. Ansell, *The Royal Mint*. 3rd edition. London, 1871.

Jayne Archer et al (eds), *The Progresses, Pageants and Entertainments of Queen Elizabeth I*. Oxford, 2007.

T. S. Ashton, *An Economic History of England: The Eighteenth Century*. London, 1955.

Edward Besly, 'A Host of Shining Angels: Money on Board the Mary Rose', *Before the Mast: Life and Death Aboard the Mary Rose*, Julie Gardiner and Michael J. Allen (eds). 2005.

Edward Besly and C. Stephen Briggs, 'Coin hoards of Charles I and the Commonwealth of England, 1625-60 from England and Wales', *British Numismatic Journal* 83 (2013).

A. Billing, *The Science of Gems, Jewels, Coins and Medals, Ancient and Modern*. London, 1867.

H. M. Boot, 'Real incomes of the British Middle Class, 1760-1850: the experience of clerks at the East India Company', *Economic History Review* 52 (1999).

Stephen Broadberry et al, *British Economic Growth, 1270-1870*. Cambridge, 2015.

I. D. Brown, 'Some notes on the coinage of Elizabeth I with special reference to her hammered silver', *British Numismatic Journal* 28 (1955-57).

I. D. Brown and Michael Dolley, *A Bibliography of Coin Hoards of Great Britain and Ireland 1500-1967*. London, 1971.

I. D. Brown and C. H. Comber, 'Notes on the gold coinage of Elizabeth I', *British Numismatic Journal* 59 (1989).

C. E. Challis, *The Tudor Coinage*. Manchester, 1978.

C. E. Challis, *Currency and the Economy in Tudor and early Stuart England*. London, 1989.

C. E. Challis (ed.), *A New History of the Royal Mint*. Cambridge, 1992.

K. N. Chaudhuri, *The Trading World of Asia and the English East India Company, 1660-1760*. Cambridge, 1978.

K. Clancy, 'The reducing machine and the last coinage of George III', *British Numismatic Journal* 70 (2000).

K. Clancy, 'The Ricardo Ingot: Experimental dies in the Royal Mint collection', *British Numismatic Journal* 71 (2001).

K. Clancy, 'The appointment of William Wellesley Pole to the Royal Mint', *British Numismatic Journal* 72 (2002).

J. H. Clapham, *An Economic History of Modern Britain, Free Trade and Steel, 1850-1886*. Cambridge, 1932.

J. H. Clapham, *The Bank of England: A History*. 2 vols. Cambridge, 1944.

B. J. Cook, 'A small sixteenth century hoard of European gold coins', *British Numismatic Journal* 62 (1992).

B. J. Cook, 'Showpieces: Medallic coins in early modern Europe', *The Medal* 26 (1995).

B. J. Cook, *Angels & Ducats: Shakespeare's money & medals*. London, 2012.

J. Craig, *The Mint. A History of the London Mint from AD287 to 1948*. Cambridge, 1953.

J. J. Cullimore Allen, *Sovereigns of the British Empire*. London, 1965.

G. Duveen and H. G. Stride, *The History of the Gold Sovereign*. London, 1962.

G. P. Dyer and M. Stocker, 'Edgar Boehm and the Jubilee coinage', *British Numismatic Journal* 54 (1984).

G. P. Dyer (ed.), *Royal Sovereign, 1489-1989*. Llantrisant, 1989.

G. P. Dyer, 'Gold, silver, and the double-florin', *British Numismatic Journal* 64 (1994).

G. P. Dyer, 'Gold and the Goschen pound note', *British Numismatic Journal* 65 (1995).

G. P. Dyer, 'Quarter-sovereigns and other small gold patterns of the mid-Victorian period', *British Numismatic Journal* 67 (1997).

G. P. Dyer, 'The Currency Crisis of 1797', *British Numismatic Journal* 72 (2002).

EEBO (Early English Books Online, http://eebo.chadwyck.com/home).

Daniel Fearon and Brian Reeds, *The Sovereign: the world's most famous coin*. 2001.

A. E. Feavearyear, *The Pound Sterling. A History of English Money*. 2nd edition. Revised by E. V. Morgan. Oxford, 1963.

F. W. Fetter, *Development of British Monetary Orthodoxy, 1797-1875*. Cambridge [Massachusetts], 1965.

Sandra K. Fischer, *Econolingua: A Glossary of Coins and Economic Language in Renaissance Drama*. 1985.

Ian Fleming, *From Russia with Love*. London, 1957.

P. Grierson, 'The origins of the English sovereign and the symbolism of the closed crown', *British Numismatic Journal* 33 (1964).

J. K. Horsefield, *British Monetary Experiments, 1650-1710*. London, 1960.

Kevin Jackson (ed.), *The Oxford Book of Money*. Oxford, 1995.

W. S. Jevons, 'On the Condition of the Metallic Currency of the United Kingdom, with reference to the Question of International Coinage', *Journal of the Statistical Society of London* (December, 1868).

W. K. Jordan, *The Chronicle and Political Papers of King Edward VI*. London, 1966.

R. Kelleher, "Gold is the strength, the sinnewes of the world': Continental gold and Tudor England', *British Numismatic Journal* 77 (2007).

E. M. Kelly, *Spanish Dollars and Silver Tokens. An account of the issues of the Bank of England 1797-1816*. London, 1976.

John Kent, *Coinage and currency in London from the London and Middlesex Records*. London, 2005.

Robert Lloyd Kenyon, *The Gold Coins of England*. London, 1884.

Eric Kerridge, *Trade and Banking in Early Modern England*. Manchester, 1988.

Jane A. Lawson, *The Elizabethan New Year's Gift Exchanges, 1559-1603*. Oxford, 2013.

Earl of Liverpool, *A Treatise on the Coins of the Realm, in a Letter to the King*. Oxford, 1805.

Michael A. Marsh, *The Gold Half-Sovereign*. Cambridge, 1982.

Michael A. Marsh, *Benedetto Pistrucci: Principal Engraver and Chief Medallist of the Royal Mint, 1783-1855*. Cambridge, 1996.

Michael A. Marsh, *The Gold Sovereign*. Cambridge, 1999.

J. B. Martin, 'Our Gold Coinage. An Inquiry into its Present Defective Condition, with a View to its Reform', *Journal of the Institute of Bankers* (June, 1882).

Peter Mathias, *The First Industrial Nation: An Economic History of Britain*. 2nd edition. London, 1983.

N. J. Mayhew, *Sterling. The Rise and Fall of a Currency*. London, 1999.

N. J. Mayhew, 'Prices in England, 1170-1750', *Past and Present* 219 (May, 2013).

D. M. Metcalf, *Sylloge of Coins of the British Isles 23, Ashmolean Museum Oxford, part III, Coins of Henry VII*. London, 1976.

Craig Muldrew, "Hard Food for Midas': Cash and its Social Value in Early Modern England'. *Past and Present* 170 (February, 2001).

E. H. Phelps Brown and Sheila V. Hopkins, 'Seven centuries of the prices of consumables, compared with builders' wage-rates', *Economica* XXIII (1956).

David Ricardo, *Proposals for an Economical and Secure Currency with Observations on the Profits of the Bank of England, etc.* London, 1816.

Thomas Snelling, *A view of the gold coin and coinage of England, from Henry III to the present time*. London, 1763.

Lord Stewartby, *English Coins, 1180-1551*. London, 2009.

C. H. V. Sutherland, *Art in Coinage: The Aesthetics of Money from Greece to the Present day*. London, 1955.

P. Villar, *A History of Gold and Money, 1450-1920*. Trans. J. White. London, 1976.

Alex Wilson and Mark Rasmussen, *English Pattern Trial and Proof Coins in Gold, 1547-1968*. Cambridge, 2000.

Peter Woodhead, *Sylloge of Coins of the British Isles 47, Herbert Schneider Collection, part I, English Gold Coins and their Imitations, 1257-1603*. London, 1996.

Peter Woodhead, *Sylloge of Coins of the British Isles 57, Herbert Schneider Collection, part II, English Gold Coins, 1603 to the 20th century*. London, 2002.

Acknowledgements

The Royal Mint Museum's Trustees commissioned this history of the gold sovereign as the first in a series of publications on the history of the British coinage. I am grateful to them and, in particular, to the Museum's former Chairman, Sarah Tebbutt, for providing the initial encouragement. The Royal Mint has also supported the project from the outset and the backing of Adam Lawrence and Shane Bissett has been extremely important in recognising the central place of history in the ongoing story of the British coinage.

My colleagues in the Royal Mint Museum, Chris Barker, Joseph Payne and Sarah Tyley have helped with assembling the images and the statistical information. The energy of Abigail Kenvyn in pursuing picture libraries and museums for the range of illustrative material included has been essential and photographers Christopher Herbert and Andrew Jenkins have worked on enhancing the book's visual aspects. Philip Skingley of Spink has generously facilitated access to several outstanding coins from the Herbert Schneider collection and I owe a debt of gratitude to the staff of the Department of Coins and Medals at the British Museum. The designer Nigel Tudman, with whom I have worked for many years, has been patient and understanding of my demands and has brought flair and good judgement to every element of the book.

It would not have been possible to attempt writing this history without access to the breadth of scholarship of Dr Joseph Bispham, Dr Christopher Challis, Dr Barrie Cook and Professor Nick Mayhew. Dr Bispham and Dr Cook very kindly read certain chapters, as have Edward Besly and my colleague Claire Hughes. Their many helpful suggestions have improved the text immeasurably. Professor Sir David Cannadine also found time to read the text and generously agreed to write the Foreword, for which I am hugely grateful. I have at different times benefitted from detailed discussions with all of them and also with Dr Martin Allen and Sir Christopher Frayling. Others have contributed constructively and in particular I would wish to thank David Baldwin, Jane Branfield, Kate Eustace, Eleanor Hoare, Professor Mark Jones, James Morton, Douglas Muir, Robin Porteous, Hazel Scott, Megan Simmonds, Anna Spender, Lord Waldegrave, the Duke of Wellington and Sir John Wheeler. Finally, I would like to thank my colleague Graham Dyer. For more years than I care to admit he has been a constant and generous source of wise counsel, unstinting rigour and, in relation to the nation's coinage, an inexhaustible source of knowledge.

Image acknowledgements